LEARNING WITHOUT LIMITS
Model Distance Education Programs in
Community Colleges

Judy Lever-Duffy
Randal A. Lemke
Larry Johnson

Editors

A joint publication of the
League for Innovation in the Community College
and the Miami-Dade Community College District

LEARNING WITHOUT LIMITS
Model Distance Education Programs in Community Colleges

Table of Contents

Table of Contents ══════════════════════

Appendix (continued)

FOREWORD

Community colleges are the higher education institutions with the orientation and flexibility to respond to a changing economy and a changing work force. They are dedicated to providing comprehensive, quality programs to diverse populations. They focus on teaching and on learning. In the Information Age, they must also focus on the delivery of quality educational programs and instructional opportunities to a work force demanding flexibility and access. This is the role that distance education can play in the community college through the application of technology.

The mission of Miami-Dade Community College is to provide accessible, affordable, high-quality education by keeping the learner's needs at the center of decision making and working in partnership with its dynamic, multicultural community. To achieve this mission now and as we look toward the twenty-first century, we must be prepared for a transformation in the way we teach, learn, and operate. We must reengineer ourselves so that we fully and effectively address the needs of our students, faculty, staff, and community. In the Information Age, this must be done through the appropriate application of technology to the teaching/learning process.

Miami-Dade Community College is currently reinventing its distance delivery systems. We have explored, created, piloted, and implemented many quality distance learning programs. But we are not content to rest upon our extensive distance education history. As the technologies change, so must we change our delivery system and the curricula it serves. I have challenged our college community to reinvent our distance education environment and build a world-class delivery system that will serve our students well into the next century. This publication and our partnership in the joint Miami-Dade Community College/League for Innovation Distance Education Project is just one aspect of this collegewide effort. We are very proud to have been a part of this project and this publication which showcases the efforts of so many fine institutions.

I look forward to seeing you on the Information Highway!

Eduardo J. Padrón
District President
Miami-Dade Community College

INTRODUCTION

Judy Lever-Duffy, Miami-Dade Community College
Randal A. Lemke, Northern Virginia Community College

Distance education has recently achieved a level of critical interest that signals a shift from the instructional periphery to mainstream instructional delivery. For years, distance education was considered experimental, even questionable, nontraditional instruction. It was often looked upon as an inferior educational option offered for those who could not participate in "real" classes.

Some of these criticisms were valid. Technologically limited distance delivery programs piloted by the early adopters of distance education often offered flexibility at the expense of sound instructional design. But the experience gained from the early innovators combined with the rampant technological advances of recent years has made it possible to expand the definition of distance education and provide a wide variety of quality educational programs.

Higher education institutions facing reduced resources and increased need for their services are turning to distance delivery in ever-increasing numbers. They recognize the massive investment by private corporations in technology-intensive distance training programs and see economic and productivity possibilities for themselves. They perceive new levels of acceptance for technology in instruction and reduced resistance by faculty and students. They are keenly aware of competition ready to use distance delivery to offer courses in their market area.

All of these forces have coalesced to put distance education in the right place, at the right time. Institutional interest is high and still growing. Educators are seeking training in, and an understanding of, distance delivery. Many institutions are trying to position themselves quickly so that they will be able to meet their student's demands before being threatened by outside competition. Distance education, once a fringe methodology, is fast becoming a fundamental methodology for the Information Age institution.

Technology has made it possible; societal and economic pressures have made it essential.

Historical Perspective

To better understand current distance education systems, a brief review of the history of those systems is useful. The terms "distance education" or "distance learning" have been used synonymously to describe a wide variety of nontraditional programs. From correspondence courses to telecourses to courses offered on the Internet, distance education has become an umbrella term to describe courses of study delivered to students in any number of nonclassroom formats. Distance education has an evolutionary history that has been influenced both by the sophistication of technology and the demand for flexible access to instruction.

Distance education began as an alternative to traditional classroom instruction in the mid-1800s. These early delivery systems, though limited by that era's technology to correspondence courses, demonstrated the same *instruction anytime, anywhere* philosophy at the core of today's distance education movement. Americans isolated in rural areas used these distance education opportunities to access education that would not have been available otherwise. Providing access to instructional opportunities has been the goal of every distance education initiative since.

While the goal has remained the same, the structure and composition of distance education has changed significantly over the years. Just as the trends and technologies in society impacted traditional education, they also altered distance education. As radio and television were adopted by the consumers, distance education programs incorporated them as well. Today, new technologies are available that have made it possible to improve the quality and ensure the variety of distance learning experiences. Many community colleges, seeking new and better ways to serve their students, have embraced distance education as a way to ensure access and promote flexible delivery of quality instruction.

Since their inception, community colleges have been at the forefront of distance education. They have effectively applied the various distance delivery approaches that have evolved throughout the history of the movement. At the same time, they have created new and innovative distance delivery formats that have improved instructional access. In a survey of American community colleges (Lever, 1991), the League for Innovation in the Community College and Miami-Dade Community College found an array of distance education approaches in place across the continent.

Each of the approaches taken by individual community colleges reflects a unique combination of formats and technologies. The study found that video technologies, including broadcast and cable TV, videocassettes, satellite uplinks and downlinks, and compressed video systems, remain the backbone of many community college programs. Many interactive video courses as well as telecourses have been developed by individual colleges or have been leased from other colleges or PBS. The study also found that audio technologies, including radio, audiocassette, and voicemail, continued to be used by many community college programs. The newest of approaches, computer and telecommunications-based systems were being incorporated into distance education programs at a growing rate. Together the print, audio, video, and computer-based approaches form the foundation of distance education efforts in community colleges today.

Regardless of the approach used, community colleges have continued to expand distance-delivered course offerings and have now begun to offer degree and certificate programs. The Annenberg/CPB Project with its *New Pathways to a Degree* program and PBS Adult Learning Services' *Going the Distance Project* have been major catalysts for the evolution from individual courses at a distance to degree programs. Recently, the League established an International Community College program that provides distance-delivered courses in partnership with Jones InterCable. Funding from state and federal governments continue to fuel distance education initiatives by contributing directly or by subsidizing the growth of the technology base needed to make new distance programming possible. Groups such as the Alfred P. Sloan Foundation, with its ambitious Asynchronous Learning Networks Project, promote the growth of distance education even further. Corporations and other private sources have joined the ranks of contributors to community college distance education initiatives as well.

The driving forces behind the explosion of interest in distance delivery, however, remain societal and technological change. The rapidly developing, easily accessed worldwide telecommunications environment has expanded the instructional world of students and faculty. The Internet and market forces that foster its growth have changed the way the society does and will do business. These forces are inexorably altering education as well. Community college students and faculty are seeking the opportunity to use existing and emerging technological tools to make instruction more accessible both on and off campus.

Distance Education in Community Colleges

Distance education is easy to recognize but more difficult to define. For the purposes of this monograph, distance education is defined as a collection of innovative approaches to the delivery of instruction to learners who are remote from their teacher. It is a process that uses a variety of technologies to overcome the time or place boundaries that separate teacher and learner. Distance education programs seek to produce the same outcomes as traditional courses, but distance programs focus on bringing that instruction to the student rather than requiring the student come to the instruction. While content and instructional goals remain the same as in traditional instruction, distance education requires that educators creatively individualize and organize the curriculum, and then use technology to deliver instruction and create opportunities for learning.

Community colleges have long sought to expand access to quality, timely instruction. Weekend colleges, independent studies, outreach programs, and facilitated learning are just a few of the many flexible formats developed by community colleges to maximize access and opportunity as economic forces and changing social roles continue to constrain community college students' time. With an average age of mid-to-late twenties, community college students typically

have significant economic responsibilities for themselves and their families. They are often working adults who want to improve their opportunities for economic success in the workplace or who require new skills to maintain their jobs. Even flexible on-campus instruction, while improving access, may not meet the needs of many community college students. For those whose life circumstance make it difficult or impossible to come to campus, distance education may be their only opportunity. For those who can come to campus for some of their courses, distance education can offer the flexibility necessary to more quickly complete degree or certificate requirements.

Distance education in community colleges is an innovative, flexible option designed to maximize access and opportunity.

Curricular Revision for Distance Delivery

The core of every distance education program is a high-quality curriculum designed specifically to meet the needs of learners remote from their instructor. Too often, in an effort to deliver a course to distance students, a faculty member's classroom presentation is video taped, duplicated, and sent to students with only minor alterations of the syllabus. The result is typically poor, both instructionally and technologically. Strategies that work well in live presentations may or may not be effective across a distance. The key is to select appropriate instructional strategies consistent with the environment in which they will be used.

Instructional design principles are as appropriate for the development of distance delivered curriculum as for classroom-based instruction. Content area goals and objectives must be identified and instructional strategies to achieve them must be selected and defined. Technologies to support the strategies must be identified. Formative and summative evaluation processes must be in place.

The differences between designing curriculum for the classroom as opposed to distance environments occur primarily in three areas. First, extra care and advance planning are necessary to select and develop strategies for learners one might never see. Second, the identification of support technologies may require extensive review and evaluation of technological options. Finally, methods for both formative and summative evaluation at a distance must be developed.

Selecting and developing instructional strategies are the most complex aspects of revising curricula for distance delivery. When teaching in a traditional format, lecture is typically the dominant instructional strategy. With a gifted teacher tuned to the verbal and visual feedback from his or her students, this can be a highly effective strategy. The master teacher in control of the classroom learning environment plans the possibilities, orchestrates events, and like the director of an interactive play, selects or rejects planned strategies as the instructional situation warrants. Good classroom instruction unfolds in rhythm with student learning.

In distance education however, instruction requires extensive choreography. Distance instruction must be meticulously planned and implemented to avoid learner confusion, frustration, or isolation. Strategies must be identified and implemented that will anticipate and address diverse learning styles. Materials must be prepared that support and expand on student reaction to the content presented. The teacher may not be present remotely or locally at the time the instruction occurs. "Real-time" instruction may be mediated by complex technology to bridge distances. In either case, the teacher does not have the option to shift strategies "on-the-fly" or try instructional alternatives as easily as is possible in the classroom. The distance educator must develop and integrate a variety of well-planned, finely tuned strategies from which students can choose as they navigate their distance learning environment. Many community college teachers have had little or no training in the process of instructional design and development of alternative instructional strategies and may require significant training and support.

Technology evaluation and selection is the second challenge for those redesigning curriculum for distance delivery. Technologies vary in complexity and availability. Simple, readily available technologies such as the telephone or fax machine can be powerful tools for distance curriculum. Few faculty, however, are trained to repurpose technologies or are supported in the process if they attempt to do so. Some technologies, when available, are complex to use, require training to achieve a comfortable operational level, and need continuous technical support. Faculty desiring to use such technologies often give up in frustration rather than struggle to integrate them into instruction. Effective distance education curricula must use support technologies to deliver content and to facilitate interaction. To that end, distance education programs must make their technologies available in a service-oriented, supportive environment. Faculty must be trained in the evaluation of technological options and in their implementation. Institutions must allocate resources not only for technology acquisition and maintenance but for support for its integration into distance learning environments.

The final area of the instructional design process that presents challenges to distance curriculum is evaluation. Formative feedback is always available in the classroom. Informal cues such as confused looks or excessive requests for clarification provide continuous feedback. Formal periodic evaluations such as quizzes and tests offer the teacher feedback throughout the instructional process. He or she is easily able to revise and adjust the instruction to respond to student needs. Formative evaluation in distance education, on the other hand, must be carefully planned for and built into the distance education curriculum. Periodic feedback points and the method used to deliver the feedback must be articulated. Summative evaluation that measures the success of the teaching/learning process is an even greater challenge. Issues of academic integrity and security are paramount. Curriculum must be designed to provide evaluation processes that assure an accurate representation of student progress.

Curricular revisions are a necessary component of distance education. The instructional design requires specific attention and revision. Overall, distance curriculum must be designed to be student-centered and student-directed. The faculty member must identify and develop strategies for content delivery that promote independent learning and self-direction. Peer-to-peer and faculty-to-student interaction should be carefully planned for and creatively facilitated in all distance education programs. In distance education, as in the traditional classroom, promoting active learning must remain a priority. Given these curriculum issues and the time and place barriers inherent in distance education, curricular revision is a necessary first step for effective distance education.

Materials and Technologies for Distance Education

Community colleges have taken a broad range of technological approaches to distance delivery. These approaches vary from delivery dominated by a single technology to those supported by multiple technologies. From the printed page to the computer screen, community college educators have found innovative applications for the full range of instructional technologies in distance delivery. An understanding of these technologies and their application is essential to the review of existing and potential distance education systems.

Every distance delivery program uses some form of the simplest and earliest distance education technology—print. Today's distance education programs use textbooks, study guides, and assignments as core materials. Materials are delivered to students by mail, and the mail system is also used to provide interaction between student and teacher. Recently, fax machines have helped to reduce response time for submission and feedback. Relatively low production costs and ease of revision are key advantages of using print in distance delivery. For faculty, the primary course development task is to create programmed learning materials that anticipate students' abilities and responses.

When used as the dominant delivery technology, however, print has significant limitations. One of the disadvantages is the dependence of this method on a single dimension for communication of the subject matter. Learning would be improved if the multidimensional experiences available in the traditional classroom could be experienced. Often, the subject matter itself requires more media to fully communicate its content. Another disadvantage is print's inability to address different learning modalities. A student may have preferred learning styles not addressed by print-based materials. A final disadvantage is the potential lack of interactivity.

Audio Technologies

Creatively applied, radio, telephone, voicemail, and audiocassettes can be effective means for conducting distance learning. Radio has been used extensively over the years to deliver real-time instruction and to promote discussion. Verduin and Clark (1991) note that for areas with low literacy rates, radio can be effective as a replacement for print. Radio broadcasts are reliable and of moderate cost. Further, instruction via radio is readily available to most students. Using a talk show format, radio can provide opportunities for students to call in and interact with each other and the instructor.

Radio, like many approaches, has limitations, however. Since radio relies on auditory delivery of content, it best addresses learners whose dominant learning mode is listening. To reach a broader range of students, it must be used in combination with some visual media. Another disadvantage of radio is one shared by all broadcast technologies—it is time-bound. Students must be available at specific broadcast times to participate or listen. Finally, radio is not student directed—that is, the student does not control the progress of the instruction. Instruction may go too fast for some and too slow for others, making it less student centered than other forms of instruction.

In contrast to radio broadcast, audiocassettes remove the time constraints from audio instruction but also eliminate opportunities for real-time interaction. Audiocassettes—easy to create and update—are a low-cost, easily distributed method of instructional delivery. They offer an opportunity to teach more comprehensive and in-depth lessons via audio technologies. Instructional units can be longer without incurring the expense of additional broadcast time. Most students have access to playback units. The recent rise in the popularity of "Talking Books" evidences the viability of this instructional technology.

The telephone is the audio-delivery technology most often underutilized. Most distance learning programs use the telephone to provide interaction and feedback between teacher and student. Far fewer use the telephone for direct instruction. Conference calling or the use of a multipoint phone bridge can provide unique opportunities for small group instruction and for teacher-directed evaluation. The limitation of this technique is inherent in all real-time instruction. To participate in telephone instruction, students are time-bound—they must be available at a given time.

In response to the time constraints of telephone conversations, voicemail has been introduced in a number of distance education programs. Voicemail is the digital version of the telephone answering machine. Its digital nature, however, offers a number of advantages. Because information is saved in digital files and can be randomly accessed, voicemail offers the possibility of programming, customizing, and selecting responses to each call. Students calling a voicemail system can select the information they wish to access and leave questions to be answered. Students can call an assigned course voicemail line at their convenience for assignments and leave specific, detailed questions for their teacher. Voicemail can also allow students to submit verbal presentations in language, speech, and other subjects where the spoken word is important to the content or the evaluation process. Faculty can also give students feedback in their individual mailboxes, further enhancing personal contact with students. By completing a voicemail assignment, every student can have the opportunity to share his or her thoughts privately and without the possibility of embarrassment in front of peers. Voicemail's disadvantage is its inability to provide lengthy instruction. It is best used for reasonably concise messages, content, and information.

Video Technologies

In contrast to the single sensory dimension offered by audio technologies, video technologies add multidimensional impact to instructional delivery to distance students. Combining visual images with audio, video technologies deliver the most life-like distance instruction. Video technologies include television, teleconferencing, compressed video, and prerecorded videocassette tapes.

Because of this, television (both broadcast and cable) has been the core technology of many distance education programs. Combining both audio and visual information into a single medium, television closely replicates a traditional classroom presentation, and faculty can broadcast their instruction to a wide audience. Just as in the classroom, commercial video can be added to enhance a lesson. Although time bound in the initial broadcast, televised instruction can be taped by the learner, making it a more flexible delivery technology. One of the main disadvantages of television is the high cost associated with production and broadcast. Further, many faculty require training to ensure their effectiveness as video instructors. This training and the subsequent direction needed when the video is created add to already high costs. Even if those costs are met, some educators have questioned the instructional value of televised teaching. Television is a passive instructional environment. Students watch and listen but do not directly participate with the instructional aides, the faculty, or with peers. The lack of interactivity is television's greatest weakness.

Teleconferencing combines live television broadcast with telephone interaction. Instruction is broadcast or cablecast and phone numbers are provided for students to call in. Students may be grouped at a remote site with a single shared phone line, or they may be scattered across the broadcast area with a personal phone line available. Combining the audio and video technologies overcomes the lack of interactivity inherent in using television alone, but since the student can communicate with the instructor via audio only, there are some limitations to faculty interaction. The teacher is often restricted to audio-only communication from the student and, lacking visual clues, may not be able to respond as comprehensively as might have been possible in person. In response to this difficulty, some programs have added an additional phone line at both teacher and student sites to support a fax machine. Students are encouraged to fax diagrams, math problems, and other questions requiring visual cues prior to calling faculty with questions.

Video conferencing uses two-way audio and video. Using a combination of digital and video technologies, it allows both teacher and students to see and hear each other in real time. Sites are directly connected through high-speed phone lines and coding/decoding (CODEC) hardware. Cameras capturing video and audio signals are set up at both the send and receive sites. Monitors are placed at both sites to enable everyone to see and hear the activity at every site. The faculty member can see students at every connected site and students at each site can see the faculty member and each other's site. Interaction is live and in real time at every location. Video conferencing most closely emulates the experience of the traditional classroom and adds to it the possibilities of interconnecting several classrooms.

One of the key disadvantages of video conferencing is cost.

Equipment must be acquired and the phone lines leased. Video conferencing rooms may need to be established if permanent facilities are desired. Additionally, technical support at both send and receive sites is necessary to reduce frustration when equipment problems occur. A second disadvantage to video conferencing is that, like traditional instruction, it is both time- and place-bound. Students need to participate at a given time and at a given place, albeit at a site that may be distant from the instructor.

Videocassettes offer a time-shifted form of video instruction. Faculty presentations are recorded on videocassettes and distributed to remote viewing sites, such as libraries or directly to the student. The videocassette format offers a more flexible approach. Students can view the instruction whenever it is convenient. Additionally, they can watch and review the instruction as many times as they need to master the material. While production costs remain high, videocassettes eliminate the broadcast costs associated with television. Videocassette reproduction is reasonably inexpensive and convenient. Most students have access to playback equipment in their homes, offices, or community libraries. Like television, video delivery is passive and not interactive when used alone.

Information Technologies

Personal computers have added a new realm to the delivery of instruction at a distance. While the older technologies had limited capacity for interaction, computers, whether stand-alone or networked, can make learning at a distance more active and can make interactivity possible. All computer-based approaches share some common disadvantages. These include the cost and availability of the computer equipment and the entry skills necessary for both faculty and student to effectively use them.

Stand-alone workstations can be used to enhance active learning through multimedia software. Such software, often authored by the faculty member, can include written material, sound, graphics, and video clips. The software can reinforce a lesson or provide direct instruction. Multimedia software is student-directed, that is, the student controls the lesson and explores the learning environment created by the faculty. Packaged multimedia lessons are stored on CD-ROM or disk and sent to distance students for use on their home or office machine.

By adding a phone line and modem to the student machine, distance delivery via telecommunications is made possible. Learners can connect to a college network and interact with faculty and peers or explore college resources. Further, if the college is connected to the Internet, the student can use the college network as a gateway to this worldwide information resource. Telecommunications and related software have several distinct applications to distance delivery, each with its own unique function.

Electronic mail allows students and faculty to send private messages to each other. This one-to-one communication provides time-shifted personal communication opportunities. Teacher and student can interact at their own convenience without making appointments to be available at the same time.

Students can interact with other students in group discussion or joint projects. Further, students can attach written assignments to their mailed messages, saving the expense and time associated with traditional mail. Return receipts can be used to ensure timely receipt and to document exchanges.

While electronic mail is time-shifted, synchronous electronic conferencing occurs in real time. Students at a distance simultaneously call in to a computer network via their computer and modem. All share a common virtual classroom wherein discussions, presentations, and questions can be shared. Although currently confined primarily to text, such interactive sessions will soon be enhanced with video and audio through the emerging software and technologies being adapted for distance delivery. This telecommunications application makes possible the addition of group assignments, teacher-led discussions, and live participation. Although time-bound, electronic conferencing overcomes isolation and promotes interactivity.

Electronic bulletin board systems (BBS), also referred to as forums, offer a one-to-many communications opportunity. These electronic spaces allow students or teachers to post messages, announcements, or responses for all to read. In distance education, these electronic bulletin boards can be used to post course information, current assignments, or to pose a discussion question. Students can, in turn, post any questions or their responses for teacher and peers to see. Other students add to the list of responses and questions. An electronic discussion ensues. The electronic BBS offers flexible, time-shifted opportunities for interaction.

Audio graphic systems combine telephone for audio exchange with shared computer-based graphic images. The student and teacher speak to each other via telephone while sharing a common image of their individual computer screens. The computer image can be jointly edited, revised, and marked up with comments or suggestions. Changes occur simultaneously on both computer screens while teacher and student discuss the lesson. A math problem can be jointly worked or an English composition corrected for grammatical errors. This technology requires one or two phone lines to each site in addition to the necessary computer hardware and software.

When the Internet is added to the capabilities of computer-based or enhanced distance learning, accessible resources and learning opportunities expand a thousandfold. Online libraries and governmental and academic databases will be easily accessible. Experts from anywhere can join a discussion or respond to e-mail. The Internet offers tremendous potential to eliminate the academic isolation associated with learning at a distance.

Synchronous and Asynchronous Learning

The technological approaches described above have coalesced into two distinct forms of distance delivery: synchronous and asynchronous. Synchronous distance education is characterized by live two-way communication. Synchronous courses are usually taught over compressed video networks, satellite downlinks with telephonic return, and audio graphic systems of computer images and voice communication. Students meet in special college facilities to participate in telecommunicated classroom instruction. There are fixed meeting times equivalent to classroom instruction and the instructional format is similar as well. The development of these courses is more time consuming than classroom course and is best done with the help of an instructional designer. Once a faculty member has taught a course in this format, however, the amount of preparation and support required in subsequent semesters is similar to an on-campus course. The only exception is the technical support needed to run the telecommunications system. Students require the same support as regular classroom students and, for the most part, they need additional means to communicate one-to-one with their instructor outside of class time and to send and receive documents. Synchronous distance education is time-bound and may be place-bound. It is the less flexible of these two broad formats.

Asynchronous distance education is characterized by intermittent, as-needed communication conducted from any location at times chosen by individual students and the faculty member. There are no fixed class times or locations and not all students are in communication at the same time with the instructor or with each other. Computer conferencing courses, telecourses, voicemail courses, and audiocassette courses are forms of asynchronous instruction. Students may never appear on campus or may infrequently come to campus to use the library, take exams, and buy books. All of their and the instructor's work is done outside the classroom. The development and support required for asynchronous courses are large and ongoing. The conversion of instructional materials from a classroom format to asynchronous learning is almost equivalent to starting over for many instructors. Instructional designers, video producers, editors, and support staff are needed to produce the extensive instructional materials needed to replace classroom lectures and discussion. The maintenance of communication between student and faculty and among students requires considerable attention. Asynchronous distance education is neither time- nor place-bound, and is the most flexible delivery system.

Classification of distance education programs according to synchronous or asynchronous delivery also defines broadly the relationship between the learner and the faculty member and provides insight into the kind and quantity of support needed. Colleges often choose between these forms to meet student needs in accord with the institution's technological resources, and according to their desire to maintain classroom-like synchronous instruction or begin offering more network-like asynchronous instruction. Many colleges that started distance learning ten or more years ago based their programs on asynchronous instruction because the technologies for synchronous education were not readily available. Now many

of these programs are adding compressed video or audio graphic technologies to conduct classroom-like instruction. Colleges that are just beginning distance education are now able to start with synchronous forms if they choose. Many, however, are selecting asynchronous learning because their students and faculty want maximum flexibility and are receptive to the application of new computer technologies, especially the Internet.

Model Programs and Practices: A National Call for Papers

In the spring of 1996, colleges across North America were invited to submit descriptions of their distance learning programs to a national panel convened by the League for Innovation and Miami-Dade Community College charged with identifying exemplary or model distance learning efforts in community colleges. The panel, which included recognized leaders in distance education from across the continent, faced a difficult task as it set about deciding which of the many colleges that submitted program abstracts would be featured in a planned publication devoted to the state-of-the-art in distance education.

This monograph is based on their recommendations. The reviewers urged us to define state-of-the-art broadly, so as to include a mix of very successful programs using both established and emerging approaches to learning at a distance. Following their suggestions, the programs described here depict a snapshot of the current landscape of community college distance education programs. The colleges detailed in the following chapters represent some of the largest and oldest distance education programs as well as some of the newest, growing programs. There is great variety in their approaches to distance education, reflecting the unique characteristics of the colleges and the communities they serve. Each featured college has a unique story to tell, and many practices worth sharing.

The 16 chapters that follow feature a single college, with each chapter organized to provide the reader with an overview of the institution, details of the distance education program at the college, and an opportunity to examine what that college considers its most unique or exemplary activity in distance delivery.

A final recommendation of the reviewers is worthy of note. The panel felt strongly that many of the colleges that submitted abstracts in the original call for proposals were extraordinary in some way. Unfortunately, space limitations prohibited the inclusion of all these worthy colleges in featured chapters, but the panel felt some recognition of the contributions of these colleges should be attempted. The editors agreed, and to that end, an annotated listing of several dozen more outstanding distance education programs is included as an appendix.

Chapter 1

AUSTIN COMMUNITY COLLEGE
Austin, Texas

Ron Brey

A college meeting the needs of its community must be responsive to the social and economic environment. It adapts programs, locations, and modes of instruction as the community changes. This has been the case of Austin Community College (ACC). In the fall of 1973, the college offered its first classes to 2,363 students in an old high school. Since then, ACC has grown to six campuses (five owned by the college), a district administrative office building, an extensive telecommunications-based distance learning program, and numerous community sites throughout its eight-county service area. More than 26,000 students attended ACC's fall 1995 semester.

Since ACC's founding, the Austin metropolitan area has doubled in population to more than one million people. The college's service area comprises a region approximately 150 miles east to west and 70 miles north to south. There is much cultural and economic diversity among the eight counties served. The ethnic diversity of the area is reflected in the ACC student body, which has over 30 percent minorities. Slightly more women than men are enrolled. Austin is a youthful community with a median age of 26 and a student average age of 27. ACC faces the opportunities and challenges of a youthful, diverse population.

Until the 1970s, Austin was dependent on the jobs created by state government and The University of Texas at Austin. While these institutions are still very important, economic growth over the past two decades has been fueled by the computer and semiconductor industries, construction, and trade. Motorola, IBM, Texas Instruments, Dell Computers, Advanced Micro Devices, Applied Materials, and many smaller companies now employ 67,000 people in manufacturing. The six percent annual employment growth in the private sector is twice that for government. ACC is constantly updating its degree programs, noncredit training, and delivery methods to serve the needs of the rapidly changing and growing local job market.

Program Overview

ACC began its distance learning program in the spring 1979 semester with two courses and 225 enrollments. The program grew steadily, but with a limited mission: to provide students in the immediate Austin area an alternative to the limited number of sections offered on campus. At that time, ACC had neither a local property tax nor its own facilities. To help meet the need of limited classroom space, the number of distance learning courses offered grew rapidly during the 1980s.

By 1990, ACC had a local tax base and was building

campuses throughout the Austin area. The number of students enrolling in distance learning classes declined. In response, the mission of the distance learning program broadened to include providing better access to courses throughout the college's eight-county service area and to meet the needs of adult learners leading busy lives. This culminated in the college's making a large commitment to distance learning telecommunications technologies. An organizational change simultaneously brought a number of different activities into the Distance Learning Office. The Distance Learning Office now is responsible for most instruction not directly under the supervision of a main campus regardless of the mode of delivery.

Students Served and Programs Offered

During the first decade of the program, the socio-economic characteristics of ACC's distance learning students were quite different from their on-campus cohorts. Over the past few years, however, distance learning and instructional telecommunications technologies have become routine experiences for more high school students and adults. This familiarity and acceptance of distance learning, coupled with the increasing demands on the time of students aged 18 to 25, has changed enrollment patterns.

Distance learning students are somewhat different from students enrolled in on-campus courses only. As compared to students enrolled in only on-campus courses, students enrolled in only distance learning courses are older and more likely to be employed full time, transfer students from another college, and white. (See Figure 1-1.)

There also is a difference among students enrolled in only distance learning courses, distance learning and on-campus courses, and only on-campus courses. Students concurrently enrolled in distance learning and on-campus courses register for the most number of credit hours—one course more than on-campus-only students. These students use the flexibility of distance learning to increase their total load during the semester.

A combination of factors lead students to enroll in distance learning courses. Students may find it difficult to attend on-campus classes due to jobs and other obligations. They are less likely to be degree-seeking students, but rather need the course for career advancement. Many on-campus sections fill early and in order to enroll in a full load of courses, students add a distance learning course in conjunction with their on-campus classes. Some courses are offered only via distance learning because of the material covered in the course and the manner in which the course is taught.

In 1995, ACC received approval from The Texas Higher Education Coordinating Board to allow students to earn any A.A., A.S., or A.A.S. degree entirely via distance learning. Because that approval is so recent, current degree options are limited to an Associate of Arts in General Studies. The number of degree options will increase within the next few years.

Campus department heads and division chairs work cooperatively to schedule a sufficient number of sections for each distance learning course to meet projected needs. Sections of distance learning courses are listed in the semester course schedule with their on-campus equivalents. Information in each course section refers students to the distance learning section in the semester course schedule. The distance learning section provides details about the program, technologies used, orientation times and locations, instructor names and telephone numbers, and course descriptions.

ACC Distance Learning Centers in surrounding counties offer a small number of classroom courses. The telecommunications-based distance learning courses are an important method by which students in these areas can take additional courses without having to come to Austin.

The need for continuing education and noncredit courses is growing rapidly, but there have been several major obstacles to offering these courses via distance learning. These include obtaining approval by accrediting organizations, funding, and gaining access to the appropriate technologies. These are being overcome, and ACC will offer its first noncredit distance learning courses during the spring 1996 semester, a series of courses designed for health care professionals requiring periodic training to retain certification.

Program Organization

The associate vice president of distance learning is responsible for the overall development and leadership of the program. This includes facilitating the process for approving and offering new courses, providing course schedule information, marketing, maintaining a student hotline, providing student access to instructional resources, assisting faculty in developing and offering courses, managing instructional telecommunications, and representing the college before public telecommunications regulatory and governmental bodies.

The Educational Television Center is a broadcast-quality television production facility with studios, edit suites, master controls, and a telecommunications center. It produces recorded programs and live televised classes, and operates cable television playback systems, two ITFS channels, satellite uplink and downlink services, and video and teleconference production services for state agencies, associations, and corporations.

Testing centers provide academic testing for distance learning and on-campus students on the six campuses and the Distance Learning Centers.

STARLINK is a video teleconference network that operates as a cooperative enterprise of Texas community and technical colleges. It serves the training, information, and distance learning needs of its members which maximize the use of existing telecommunications technologies and production facilities. STARLINK is comanaged by ACC and the Dallas County Community College District.

The Distance Learning Office is part of academic affairs and reports to the executive vice president of Academic Affairs. All credit and noncredit instructional activities and the campus vice presidents are part of academic affairs. This structure provides comprehensive and unified planning, implementation, and management of instructional activities.

The policies and procedures for assigning faculty, loading, and compensation are similar to those for on-campus instruction. Faculty volunteer to teach distance learning sections. A faculty member may be requested to teach a

Figure 1-1: **Fall 1995 Semester Enrollment Patterns**

	Distance Learning Courses Only	Distance Learning & On-Campus Courses	On-Campus Only
No. of Students	1,022	1,786	22,016
Credit Hours Enrolled	5.1	10.6	7.7
Average Age	29.0	26.3	22.0
Employment			
Full-Time	55.7%	44.5%	48.9%
Part-Time	14.6%	22.7%	20.9%
Seeking Work	11.1%	9.6%	8.9%
Admissions			
High School	24.8%	36.5%	44.2%
GED	3.1%	7.5%	7.5%
Transfer	69.9%	53.8%	45.6%
Ethnicity			
White	72.4%	70.9%	67.8%
Hispanic	11.8%	16.3%	18.5%
Black	7.7%	5.9%	6.3%

distance learning course when, at the last minute, an instructor cannot teach and a substitute must be found. Assignments for distance learning sections are made in the same way as on-campus sections, and are the responsibility of department heads and division chairs.

Over 80 percent of the distance learning sections are taught by full-time faculty, compared to 35 percent of on-campus sections. Part-time faculty may teach distance learning sections, but full-time faculty have first choice. All distance learning faculty report to their usual department head or division chair. Contracts, evaluations, and related issues are handled by department heads or division chairs.

Funding for the distance learning program and activities is identical to other academic programs. The annual budget is developed and approved along with the others in academic affairs. Funding is from the college's general fund. The Distance Learning Office, however, has an enterprise account which is used for contract services. Net income is used to support the development of instructional materials for distance learning courses, faculty development, video productions, and equipment purchases.

The distance learning program is a cost-effective means of delivering instruction even with the additional telecommunications costs. More importantly, the average number of students enrolled in a distance learning class is about 30 while for on-campus sections it is 20. This results from the usual procedure of filling one section of a distance learning course before a new one is offered.

Instructional Strategies

In 1979, the distance learning program used two instructional strategies—recorded telecourses and print-based courses. Recorded telecourses were leased from producers. Print-based courses used textbooks. Over the years, the number of technologies used to provide access to distance learning courses increased. The philosophy of the ACC distance learning program is that faculty adapt courses to distance learning by using the technologies that they believe are the most appropriate for the courses and students. Although the course schedule lists five distinct types of distance learning courses, there is, in fact, a wider variety ranging from print-only to totally online via a personal computer with a modem. All five types of courses use textbooks.

Telecourses use recorded video programs. Most are acquired from other institutions, although ACC has produced several for its own use, e.g., Art History I. Students may view the programs at home on cable television, in ACC libraries and Distance Learning Centers, or rent a set of tapes for the semester.

Live televised classes originate at the Pinnacle Campus and are viewed by students at home on cable television. Students can call in questions during the class. Before teaching a live course for the first time, a faculty member receives training on how the technology can be used effectively and then works with a television director to adapt the course to this delivery method.

E-mail and Internet courses require students to have access to a personal computer with a modem. Internet-based courses

have generated considerable faculty interest. Traditionally, the Distance Learning Office has worked with faculty on a one-on-one basis to develop the courses. However, during the spring 1996 semester, 70 faculty attended an introductory workshop on the Internet and distance learning. Twenty faculty will be selected, based on project proposals, to go through an intensive seven-week training process.

Print-based courses relying on textbooks have been an important part of the distance learning program since its inception, but these are rapidly incorporating other technologies. Many use audiotapes, video programs, and the Internet as supplementary activities.

Directed-study courses are offered on a limited basis. These require students to spend time at a social service, health, or government institution as a major part of their coursework.

All new distance learning courses must be approved by the appropriate collegewide instructional task force. The approval form is an agreement between the Distance Learning Office and the faculty. It describes the course's proposed instructional activities, materials, and support services. Faculty are encouraged to meet with distance learning and other college staff on how to adapt courses for distance learning. The result is a proposal which describes faculty and staff activities before the course is offered the first time, the resources to be made available, and who will provide them.

ACC has several offices that support faculty development activities for distance learning. The Distance Learning Office works with faculty on an individual basis, hires outside experts to make presentations, and sends faculty to workshops and conferences. The LRS Instructional Development staff provide expertise on certain topics and activities that it supports; e.g., use of the Internet. The Educational Catalyst Center (EC[2]) has staff and resources to assist faculty with major instructional design and development projects. EC^2 helps faculty assemble resources from different offices located throughout the college.

The care taken in the development and approval process is one of the most important reasons for the long-term success of ACC's distance learning program. The process and college policies make it clear that faculty responsibilities for course content, instructional activities, and student grading are the same for distance learning as for on-campus courses. Key provisions of the approval form are: the type of distance learning course and technologies to be used; the rationale for offering the course; the instructional materials to be acquired and produced before the course is offered; the activities of the instructor and distance learning office before offering the course; the compensation, if any, the instructor will receive for preparing the course; the loading (number of students per section); and any funds for an assistant.

The advent of low-cost, powerful, interactive technologies is perhaps the single most important innovation in distance learning over the past decade. ACC, along with many other colleges, is making the transition from limited options for student interaction with the instructor and fellow students to one where communications can occur almost at any time.

Real-time communications have been limited to telephones used to call instructors in their offices or to pose questions during live classes shown on cable television. In either case, students must follow a schedule to communicate. This is a limitation for many students who have work and other commitments that conflict with the primary reasons why students enroll in ACC distance learning courses. Electronic bulletin board systems and the Internet are significant new methods of synchronous real-time telecommunications. ACC hopes to add this important tool to all distance learning classes in 1996.

Instructional communications have often been associated with slowness and inefficiencies—"telephone tag" and "snail mail." Voicemail and pagers are improvements but have limited instructional applications. The Internet is a powerful new tool for asynchronous and synchronous communications—and not just for its text capabilities, but for its ability to transmit graphics and pictures, online conversations, and increasingly provide access to video and audio. ACC is striving to provide video-on-demand and multimedia via high-speed data lines. The Internet, video-on-demand, and multimedia will be key components of many new courses and will be incorporated into existing ones.

Technologies Employed

The distance learning program is responsible for most instructional telecommunications technologies at ACC. ACC has an educational access channel on cable television systems serving more than 20 communities and 220,000 subscribers. Two ITFS channels are collocated with the local wireless cable system, serving more than 11,000 subscribers in a five-county area. One channel is used for recorded telecourses and live, televised classes. This programming is retransmitted by cable companies outside the Austin area and received by 40,000 subscribers. The second channel is used for programs within ACC campuses and centers, teleconferences, and contract training for businesses. Television production facilities originate live televised classes that are shown on cable television systems. Also, videotapes of all recorded telecourses are available in all ACC campus libraries and Distance Learning Centers, and students may rent tapes for the semester.

Some online courses use an academic department's own server and bulletin board or e-mail systems. Increasingly the Internet is being used for online courses. With the completion of ACCNET in 1996, students will be able to use computers in labs and libraries throughout the district to access e-mail accounts and files.

ACC is a member of the Greater Austin Area Telecommunications Network (GAATN), an interlocal agency with seven members. In addition to ACC, these political subdivisions of the state include: the Austin Independent School District, the City of Austin, Travis County, the State of Texas, the Lower Colorado River Authority, and The University of Texas at Austin. Each member owns its own fibers in all or part of the 285-mile network. Construction was completed in February 1996. ACC uses the network for voice (1995), a high-speed ATM data network (1996), and digital and analog video at a later date. The network will allow GAATN member employees and the

public to access instructional and support services at the 300-plus sites on the network.

The direction of these technological implementations has been from noninteractive, recorded, scheduled media to those which are interactive (synchronous and asynchronous) and which provide access to instructional resources on demand. ACC staff believe that the highest student success and satisfaction in distance learning courses occurs with technologies that allow students control over the telecommunications to access instructional resources.

Student Services Provided

ACC and the Distance Learning Office are committed to providing distance learning students equal access to instructional and administrative support services. Technological innovations have improved access to these services, but have also required continual adaptation and development.

The new-student admissions process is the same for distance learning and on-campus students. Most new students take a computerized placement test and meet with advisors to review career goals and plans. Then students use the same telephone registration process for on-campus and distance learning sections.

At orientation sessions, distance learning students receive a packet from the LRS that explains library services. These services include direct dialing to the electronic catalog system or contacting the Distance Learning Librarian via an 800 number. Books and reference materials can be delivered either to a student's home or to a Distance Learning Center.

Textbooks, software and other instructional materials may be purchased at a campus bookstore, distance learning center, or by mail with a credit card.

Students may call a hotline for information about courses, resource materials, orientation information, or for any other assistance with the registration process. The Distance Learning Office also assists students, either resolving any issue or forwarding it to the appropriate person (e.g., faculty on grading). Staff then follow the process to ensure that it is resolved.

Student Grading and Program Evaluation

Faculty are responsible for designing the standards to measure student success. These may include monitored exams, essays, papers, computer programs, one-on-one sessions with faculty or assistants, and other activities deemed appropriate. Monitored exams are given in testing centers. In most courses, at least five exams and/or other activities are used to determine student grades.

Evaluation of the distance learning courses and faculty assessment follow general college policy. A questionnaire is completed by students that assesses all aspects of instruction and support services. A slightly different version of the on-campus questionnaire is used for distance learning courses. Data are submitted to the appropriate instructional and support services administrators as part of the annual assessment and evaluation process. Administrators working with faculty are responsible for bringing about appropriate changes and improvements based on these data.

A more extensive distance learning program evaluation is performed once every several years. This includes an analysis of successful completion rates and grade distribution. Outside consultants may be hired to assist in a more in-depth program evaluation.

The evaluation processes identify instructional materials, delivery systems, and support services that need to be changed or improved. The Distance Learning Office assists throughout the evaluation processes. The appropriate instructional or support service office, however, is responsible for implementing any action.

Unique or Exemplary Practices

One of the strongest features of ACC's program is the Texas-wide video teleconference network, STARLINK, which began operating in the fall of 1989 with a Carl Perkins grant from the Texas Higher Education Coordinating Board. Its original mission was to deliver professional development to technical and vocational faculty of Texas community and technical colleges. Since then, STARLINK has expanded its professional development programming to include academic faculty and administrators. The board now uses STARLINK as an effective medium for communicating policy updates and other information important to Texas two-year colleges. Since 1990, STARLINK has cooperated with state agencies to address employee training needs by working on a contractual basis to produce teleconferences and arrange receive sites at member colleges. STARLINK is currently poised to play a facilitating role in planning and implementing distance learning technology among Texas two-year colleges. STARLINK owns none of the telecommunications infrastructure it uses, but rather, maximizes the use of its member colleges' technology, commercial facilities, and the state government's telecommunications infrastructure. STARLINK is managed by Austin Community College and the Dallas County Community College District on behalf of community and technical colleges throughout Texas with the guidance of a statewide advisory committee and an executive council.

The Distance Learning Office also provides contract video and teleconference services for governmental agencies, professional associations, and the private sector through its Educational Television Center. During the past year, dozens of teleconferences were produced to provide client staff and members throughout the state with training and information. This is a rapidly growing activity and is an important source of funds used to support the distance learning program.

Recently, ACC has signed a memorandum of understanding with Secure Digital Communications, Inc. (SDC), to develop, market, and deliver multimedia content via state-of-the-art telecommunications technologies. Working with corporate partners such as Incite and National Semiconductor, SDC will deploy networked multimedia labs and stand-alone personal computers using isochronous IEEE 802.9a, isoEthernet technology. Over a three-year period, the project will grow from stand-alone multimedia labs, to using GAATN to tie together labs at several ACC campuses, and then to student homes and businesses via ISDN and other high-speed networks. This technology will be able to provide:

- just-in-time training to industries and government;
- videoconferencing;
- multimedia mail;
- remote presentations;
- instructional help desk services and tutoring;
- multimedia and video-on-demand file servers to access LRS resources;
- narrowcast real-time video and interconnection to cable and broadcast television systems;
- desktop collaboration;
- digital multimedia production, editing, and animation; and
- collaborative curriculum development among staff and faculty at various sites.

The ingredients to develop a successful distance learning program vary from college to college. During the first decade of its program, ACC had the right combination of faculty and administrative support, a reasonable faculty loading formula, faculty responsibility and control over the courses offered, the resources to develop courses, a clear market demand, and an evolutionary approach. During the past several years, however, additional ingredients have been added as Austin emerged as a high-tech community. The distance learning program has faced challenges due to changes in the economy, the need for ongoing training due to heightened competition and employment insecurity, and the dissemination of new computer and telecommunications technologies. ACC is meeting these challenges by continuing to invest in innovative technologies to support distance learning and to improve the quality of the program. ACC's goal is to provide high-quality credit courses and noncredit training when and where students want it.

Ron Brey
Associate Vice President, Distance Learning
Austin Community College – Pinnacle Campus
7748 Highway 290 West
Austin, TX 78736-3290
(512) 223-8028; fax: (512) 288-8111
e-mail: rbrey@austin.cc.tx.us

Chapter 2

CHATTANOOGA STATE TECHNICAL COMMUNITY COLLEGE
Chattanooga, Tennessee

Sue Y. Hyatt

Chattanooga State Technical Community College in Chattanooga, Tennessee, is the largest of the community colleges in the Tennessee Board of Regents System. Located in the extreme southeastern corner of the state and bordering Alabama and Georgia, the college serves one urban county and four rural counties in Tennessee and rural counties in Alabama and Georgia. The assigned service area of the college extends for approximately 150 miles north-to-south and approximately 75 miles east-to-west across mountainous terrain and two different time zones, though the area served by the Distance Learning Program includes the entire state of Tennessee as well as areas of the three border states. A truly comprehensive college, Chattanooga State has an enrollment of approximately 10,000 students in both career and transfer two-year degree programs as well as one-year vocational certificates and an applied technology degree which merges vocational preparation with a one-year core of college-level courses.

As in most community colleges nationwide, the typical student is a 26-year-old female who works at least part-time, has a family, and may live as far as 75 miles away from the college.

Program Overview

As early as 1976, Chattanooga State was beginning to teach an occasional course on "Sunrise Semester" through the local Public Broadcast affiliate. The college was also videotaping selected classes to allow students to review problematic course content in a lab setting. By 1979, a decision was made to create a "learning lab" which would serve three purposes: 1) to provide testing services for the college, including the college placement test, make-up examinations, and credit-by-examination tests; 2) to videotape classes for student review; and 3) to offer lab-based video courses. Within a year, the college was offering six lab-based independent-study courses, of which four were preproduced and licensed courses and two were developed in-house.

By 1985, the college had built an Instructional Television Fixed Service (ITFS) system to broadcast live instruction from the campus to high school sites in three rural counties. At its height, this system transmitted as many as eight courses per semester into as many as six locations. Also in 1985, the college began to offer three to four courses on the Public Broadcast System each semester while continuing to increase the number of lab-based videotaped courses.

In 1989, the decision was made to make telecourses available to students at home via videotapes checked out in person or mailed. This new approach, the Video Instruction Program (VIP) ushered in a period of rapid growth in terms of both student enrollments and the number of courses offered. In 1990, all the different transmission modes were united under one administrative department: Distance Learning. Since that time, online courses have been added and the college is experimenting with the use of desktop videoconferencing for delivery of some types of instruction as well as for selected student services. By 1997–98, the college will be able to broadcast live instruction into homes in the rural areas of its region through a partnership with a wireless cable company using a microwave multipoint distribution system (MMDS).

Perhaps the most unique characteristic of the program is its diversity in terms delivery systems used, types of courses offered, and a commitment to try new ways to accommodate student's needs and interests.

Students Served and Programs Offered

In the spring of 1995 an analysis was done to see where students enrolled in distance learning courses in the fall and spring semesters lived. A total of 2,493 enrollments were reviewed, and two distinct patterns emerged as outlined below:

- Immediate Chattanooga area: 1438 (57.8%)
- Other distant city clusters: 281 (11.2%)
- Scattered rural areas: 774 (31.0%)

The rural areas were spread all across the state of Tennessee, extending from the border with Virginia to a small town near Atlanta, Georgia; from Bowling Green, Kentucky, to northeastern Alabama, and all the way to Memphis.

The 2,493 enrollments represent 1,628 actual individuals. In many cases, these students were enrolling in distance learning classes in addition to traditional classes. They were probably seeking to accelerate their progress through their degree programs. In other cases, students were likely to be taking these courses because the traditional lecture class was either closed due to low enrollment or overfilled. However, 512 of the enrollments (20.5 percent) represented students who were taking only distance learning courses. Therefore, it is reasonable to assume that these students were only able to access the college through the Distance Learning Program.

Perhaps the most unusual group of students served by the program were some 70 inmates at a regional men's prison located 75 miles from the campus. In the last two years before the revocation of the Pell grant for prisoners, eight men were able to complete enough courses through a combination of ITFS, on-site, and distance learning instruction to receive A.S. degrees.

A survey of students enrolled in distance learning courses in 1993 listed the following reasons for enrolling:

- Convenience   48.6%
- Time Factors   30.9%
- Learning Style   8.4%
- Course Content   7.9%
- Other   4.2%

While the average percentage of distance learning students taking only one distance learning course in a given semester is usually between 45 and 55 percent, it is not unusual to find a small number of students who take three or more distance learning courses per semester. Some Chattanooga State graduates have completed as many as 15 distance learning courses.

Over the years, the Distance Learning Program has served home-bound students, prisoners, expectant and new mothers, swing-shift workers, and others. Serving this diverse clientele has brought about some creative course development. For example, the instructional units for Anatomy and Physiology I and II, which are key courses for all the Allied Health programs, have been videotaped cooperatively by all the full-time course instructors for student use at home. Generally, these students must sign up for an on-campus lab at the time of their choice. However, in two notable incidents, students have had to arrange to take the labs on a rotating basis due to shifting work schedules and the fact that they held down two jobs. Fortunately, the program was able to accommodate these students, and both passed the courses.

At present, the VIP (check-out/mail-out option) offers 73 courses across the following curriculum areas:

- Allied Health   6 courses
- Biological/Natural Sciences   10 courses
- Business/Information Science   12 courses
- Career/Study Skills   2 courses
- Liberal Arts   34 courses
- Mathematics   9 courses

In addition, a variety of other courses, including all the developmental review courses, have been taught via the college's "live" one-way video/two-way audio broadcast system. Also four to six courses are broadcast each fall and spring semester on the education channel of the local television cable company. Finally, eight courses have been taught online, using either a national online service or a local Internet provider. Instructional design for these courses has varied from primarily e-mail interchange between students and faculty to weekly two-hour "live" online discussions including "guest speakers."

At this time, CSTCC is developing the courses for three certificates in the areas of Arboriculture, Forestry, and Fire Science Administration. The Fire Science Administration courses will also form the basis of a new two-year degree concentration, which will be offered completely through distance learning. In addition, the Weekend College degree program in Management includes one distance learning course paired with two traditional courses taught on the weekend as part of its program each semester.

The courses taught through videotape check-out/mail-out comprise over 85 percent of the total distance learning enrollments. Approximately half of the courses in the program are preproduced, licensed telecourses. The other 50 percent have been developed on the Chattanooga State campus by faculty members in conjunction with the college's Media Services Center.

Program Organization

Currently serving approximately 3,000 students each year, the Distance Learning Program is staffed by a full-time director, a part-time assistant director, three clerical employees, and a temporary part-time worker assigned to special projects. The program reports directly to the vice president for Institutional Advancement, who is also responsible for campus computing functions, fund raising, institutional research, continuing education, marketing, telecommunications, and media.

Curriculum for the program is determined jointly by the distance learning program director and the deans and department heads. All courses are reviewed by the campus curriculum committee and approved by the vice president for academic affairs. Faculty who develop courses for the program receive extra compensation based the amount of work and the complexity of the project. In addition, in cases where a great deal of time and effort are required to do a project, release time is given as well. Compensation for course development is made through line items in the program budget. All costs associated with the program are funded through the regular budget cycle of the college. For the past two years, the program has achieved a cost/benefit ratio in which benefits have outstripped costs by a margin of two to one.

With approval of the program director, instructors are chosen and paid by the departments offering courses. (These are usually the course developers.) In the fall semester of 1995, over 85 percent of the instructors teaching distance learning courses were full-time faculty members, and this number included six department heads and one academic dean. The ratio of full-time to part-time faculty teaching these courses varies from term to term but very rarely goes below 70-percent full-time.

While most of the courses offered through the program fall within the general core courses of the college, more discipline-specific courses are being developed to meet the perceived needs of individual programs or departments. In addition, some courses, such as those in the Forestry certificate program, have been developed at the request of contracting industries which need training for their workers.

Instructional Strategies

Perhaps the most outstanding feature of the program at Chattanooga State is the breadth and variety of the course offerings and the range of technologies used to reach students. During earlier periods of the program, much emphasis was placed on synchronous learning through the "live" broadcast ITFS option. Over the past three years, however, the emphasis has definitely shifted to asynchronous modes to follow very obvious enrollment trends. Before the introduction of the videocassette check-out/mail-out option, enrollments in ITFS were higher than in the lab-based telecourse program. However, since 1991, ITFS enrollments dropped from a high of 364 to just 31 in 1994–95, while enrollments in the Video Instruction Program rose from 1,835 in 1991 to 2,805 in 1994–95.

Despite the high popularity of asynchronous learning, the introduction of online courses in 1994–95 has opened up a new avenue for both "real-time" and "time-shifted" interchange for distant learners and instructors. Five courses are currently offered which allow instructor and students to engage in online dialogue with each other and with other students, as well as to interact individually through e-mail. Two of the instructors have designated specific times for students to "meet" in online chat rooms for discussion, much as they would do in an on-campus seminar setting. Satisfaction with this mix of synchronous and asynchronous instruction is steadily increasing, and instructors are beginning to view this type of delivery as a positive and interesting new way to teach students.

Over the past several years, some aspects of course design for distance learning courses have remained the same, while others have been steadily changing. From the outset of the program, it was decided that there should be a "mix" of objective and subjective assignments for most nonmathematics courses. Including assignments that can be easily graded by lab workers provides students with quick feedback about course performance and helps keep them involved in doing the work.

For students to progress to higher understanding of subject matter, however, they must be required to do more than parrot back information provided by the textbook, the videotape, or the instructor. As a result, almost all courses have included at least one paper or one fairly substantial project. Increasingly, students are being asked to use their own communities as research labs to perform such tasks as designing a small business as part of an introductory business course, writing to legislators or attending a town council meeting for students in government class, or observing children or patients in a mental health facility for students in psychology classes. Through such instructional strategies, students can merge the information they are learning in the course with practical applications in the "real world." This blending of emphasis on learning specific concepts, terms, and ideas with a synthesis and integration of ideas into a larger framework strengthens the learning experience for distance learners and works to overcome the solitude inherent in this type of learning experience.

Technologies Employed

The dominant technology for serving students through distance learning at this time is videocassette check-out/mail-out. Courses are also broadcast each spring and fall over the public education channel of the local cable television company. Five online courses are presently being offered, with an additional three courses expected to be operational in the spring of 1997. Two of the online courses include videotapes as part of the delivery system.

At present, Chattanooga State is not offering courses via "live" broadcast modes due to the age of the system and the increasing growth of satellite campuses in two of its service counties. A contract has been signed, however, with a company that will make "live" in-home instruction available to prospective students in rural areas through a microwave multipoint distribution system (MMDS). In addition, the college has installed a desktop videoconferencing system which will allow students at the two remote satellite campuses to receive tutoring, advising, and small group instruction in a "live" interactive manner via computers. This technology allows two-way video, two-way audio, and document sharing. It may also be used both synchronously and asynchronously. With funds provided by a grant, this same technology is scheduled to be installed between the main campus and two small manufacturing companies in order to provide on-site training for company employees.

The director of Distance Learning is responsible for providing training sessions for faculty using these technologies. The coordinator of Academic Media Services has developed an online course which serves the dual purposes of illustrating how a well-designed online course is designed and teaching faculty and staff to use common tools for mining the Internet. Technical assistance is provided by personnel in the media center and the Computer Services areas.

Student Services Provided

Students taking distance learning courses receive the same services as students taking classes on the campus. They may avail themselves of advising/counseling services either in person, at off-campus sites, or by telephone. They may register at off-campus sites, on the main campus, or, in some cases, by telephone. Students may request books or other resource information by mail or fax from the Chattanooga State Library or through interlibrary loans. Students may call on instructors in person, by telephone, or via e-mail. Instructors are expected to keep regular office hours to assist these students and to provide tutoring services if they are needed. Distance learning students are also welcome to all student activities, honors, and special programs of the college. Added services for these students include a daily "pony" from the main campus to the outlying campuses, arrangements for ordering books by telephone from the bookstore, and visits twice each semester by the assistant director to staff members at three remote prison sites.

Student Grading and Program Evaluation

The same grading standards apply to distance learning students as in all regular on-campus courses. All courses require at least a midterm and a final examination, and all nonmathematics courses require at least one paper or project. Most courses require both objective tests and subjective evaluation. Distance learning students may request additional time to complete course work if they have already completed at least one half of the work required.

The syllabus packets that students receive upon enrolling in distance learning courses include a brief course evaluation form to be completed at the end of the course. In addition, a more formal evaluation survey is mailed to all students enrolling in distance learning classes once each year. Faculty members who teach distance learning courses are also surveyed to determine their satisfaction with the courses and the program, and their input for change is solicited.

Statistics are gathered about student performance each semester, and an overall annual assessment of student performance and retention, as well as performance in individual courses across instructors, is made each year. Comparison of student performance in comparable traditional courses is also reviewed. Based on these assessments, changes are made to address issues raised.

Unique or Exemplary Practices

Perhaps the strongest aspect of the program lies in its unusual degree of interactivity as a bridge between the students and instructors. While the various departments of the college select the faculty who develop and instruct distance learning courses, the program provides a broad range of services to both faculty and students.

A handbook is provided for both course developers and instructors teaching courses for the first time. This handbook offers guidance in writing good syllabi for distance learning courses and good information about how these courses usually work. All syllabi are reviewed each semester to be sure that weekly activities and assignments are spelled out clearly so that students know what is expected and approximately when weekly activities and assignments are due. Instructors must "think ahead" to determine what information students must have if they are to do the work expected of them.

Often, including good examples illustrating the work required as part of the syllabus package makes the difference between a student who continues in the course and one who gives up in frustration. Examples of such assistance include a copy of an excellent summary of an article or video, including citations, or an introductory videotape to explain in detail how to get started in developing a business plan. Program staff are responsible for getting the syllabus printed, assembled, and bar-coded for check-out to students at or before the beginning of each semester.

Perhaps the most unique aspect of the program is that all coursework is routed through the program office. Course materials are sent out from the program office, and student work is returned there as well. All work (with the exception of online work) which enters or leaves the office is logged in to provide a record of both student and faculty activity. Objective exams are graded immediately by program staff so that students receive immediate feedback, and papers requiring faculty evaluation are distributed to each instructor daily. When the work has been graded by the faculty, it is returned to the program office, where the results are entered into each student's file. Then the program staff notify the student of his results, by mailing back the paper itself or an errata sheet which shows the grade and any errors that were made.

The program also sends standard mailings to the students,

such as "you are behind" letters giving the final date to withdraw, and the procedures for withdrawing if the student feels catching up is impossible. Program staff mail out any correspondence instructors wish to send to students. In addition, the director assists instructors in averaging student grades at the end of the term, if they so desire.

While these practices are time consuming and labor intensive, they fulfill two important functions. First, students are assured of having a backup regarding work they have turned in. Instructors are protected since the program office records all work returned to students. Equally important, however, this interaction provides the director with information about how students are progressing, as well as how efficiently instructors are providing feedback to students, a factor found critical in keeping students actively working to complete courses. While these services are not universally well received by faculty, students express great appreciation for them.

Finally, the willingness to adapt instruction to a variety of situations has been a key factor in the growth of the program. Examples include finding ways to provide on-site labs for prisoners taking lab science courses, providing oral testing for students with special needs, and arranging for proctoring of tests at approved off-site locations. The program currently serves power-line maintenance personnel scattered in isolated pockets all over the Tennessee Valley. Their examinations are proctored by the training officer in their location or by their supervisor. Twenty-two staff members of two regional prisons located some 200 miles from the college are proctored by the director of educational programs at each prison under a dual-services agreement with the state of Tennessee.

Perhaps the most interesting new challenge is how to handle the examinations for over-the-road truck drivers who are taking a newly developed one-year certificate in highway transportation business. As the program becomes more fully integrated into company training efforts, additional procedures will have to be developed, but such new alliances will provide new enrollments for the college and new opportunities for students who might otherwise not be able to access higher education.

Attention to detail and to student needs, providing assistance to faculty involved with the program, and finding new ways to reach students have been the keys to the success of this program. As long as students find courses they need, enjoy the convenience they require, and receive the services they deserve, the program the college will continue to grow.

Sue Hyatt
Director of Distance Learning
Chattanooga State Technical Community College
4501 Amnicola Highway
Chattanooga, TN 37406
(423) 697-4408; fax: (423) 697-4479
e-mail: Hyatt@cstcc.cc.tn.us

Chapter 3

CHEMEKETA COMMUNITY COLLEGE
Salem, Oregon

Donna Carver and Janet King

Begun in 1955 as Salem Technical Vocational School, the Chemeketa Community College district was formed in September 1969. Chemeketa is a comprehensive community college employing approximately 250 full-time faculty members and offering professional-technical education, college transfer courses, developmental skill-building classes, and lifelong learning opportunities. The FTE for 1994–1995 stands at 9,051 with about 40,000 students enrolling in Chemeketa classes and workshops every year; nearly 3,500 enroll full-time each term.

The Chemeketa Community College district covers more than 2,600 square miles in Oregon's mid-Willamette Valley, encompassing three counties and part of a fourth. The main campus is located in Salem, the state capitol; there are college centers in four communities located throughout the district. Specific distance education courses have been designed to serve students at these centers and inmates at two correctional facilities in Salem.

Chemeketa's first distance education class, a telecourse, was offered in the spring of 1979 on broadcast television. The class was offered as a joint effort between members of the Oregon Community College Distance Education Consortium and Oregon Public Broadcasting. Distance education at Chemeketa today combines the technologies of television, prerecorded and live; cable and satellite; correspondence; and computers. In some cases, courses are designed to be offered by specific technologies; in other cases, a combination of technologies is used.

In the fall term of 1994, the college began to offer the Associate of Arts Oregon Transfer, the Associate of General Studies, and the Associate of Applied Science in Fire Protection degrees, as well as noncredit and professional technical classes via distance education technologies. Currently, 50 to 60 distance education courses are offered each term and the college enrolls approximately 4,000 students each academic year in some form of distance learning class.

At Chemeketa, the use of distance education technologies is valued as a vital part of the overall mix of learning choices provided to students. These technologies are no longer peripheral or experimental, but have become an integral part of how education is delivered. Distance education is an imperative for the college's continued viability, and the college is increasing its flexibility in meeting the lifelong learning needs of students.

Program Overview

Students Served and Programs Offered

There is not a "typical" student at Chemeketa. Recent high school graduates attend class with retired grandparents; they all come to the college with diverse goals and expectations. Some students attend full-time, others part-time, and many combine work with school. Some students combine traditional campus-based classes with distance education classes to meet their needs. Typically, students who enroll in distance education classes attend part-time, are older and employed, and most bring college credits with them when they begin their pursuit of a degree through the distance education option. It has been found that students who are successful in these classes are independent self-starters.

Chemeketa's distance education programs are designed with the flexibility to accommodate students of any age and life situation by bringing education to the students at times and locations that fit their varied schedules and lifestyles. These students may have difficulty in attending class at a set time or location for a number of reasons, which may include distance from a college facility, personal and employment commitments, or disabilities. Distance education courses eliminate these barriers and provide students with the opportunity to earn a degree while pursuing career and personal goals. Students enrolled in these courses experience practical applications of information age technologies. For potential students who are unable to fit a typical college schedule into their lives, distance education is an innovative solution that makes up-to-date education affordable and accessible. Chemeketa regards distance education as a means of providing learning opportunities to students who would not otherwise access college services.

Whatever students' goals and interests, the college is committed to their educational success. In recognition of the needs of lifelong learners, the college is partnering with several higher education institutions in Oregon to make a four-year degree available to students via distance education on completion of a Chemeketa two-year degree.

Program Organization

The college vision states that "Chemeketa is a dynamic community of learners and innovators. Undaunted by limitations, we seek to improve the quality of life for individuals, our community, and the world."

As the vision statement illustrates, Chemeketa places a high value on the creativity of its employees; faculty and staff are encouraged to take risks and explore innovative ideas. To this end, the college provides numerous opportunities for staff to receive funding, release time, travel and writing opportunities, and personal recognition for the development and implementation of exemplary practices.

The college collaborates with local employers to ensure

that Chemeketa graduates have the skills necessary to enter the job market. The college has found that employers are looking for employees who not only have job-specific skills, but have the skills needed to compete in this age of information and technology. Moreover, students expect and deserve to have marketable skills as well as a degree when they graduate. By participating in distance education classes, students gain experience using information age technology, as well as skills in information finding and critical thinking.

A successful distance education program requires a champion. Over the years, Chemeketa's champions have inspired enthusiasm for using technology as an instructional delivery method and have been the impetus behind distance education becoming a part of mainstream instruction. It would not be possible to deliver degrees via distance education without the support and collaboration of the entire Chemeketa community.

Political commitment at state and institutional levels is necessary to garner needed resources and to promote a continuing dialog among key players. The institution must have a commitment to identifying unserved student populations and be determined to find ways of overcoming barriers to education for these students.

College administrators, faculty who teach the courses, technicians, and support staff are committed to delivering quality distance education courses and assume collective responsibility for the program's success. Specific responsibility for the delivery of distance education programs lies with the director of the Learning Resource Center and the director of Chemeketa Online.

The distance education coordinator in the Learning Resource Center provides a single point of access to information for students and faculty. The coordinator is responsible for a multitude of tasks, including course recommendation and scheduling, planning and budgeting, copyright compliance, keeping technologies current, and working with college departments and colleagues at other colleges to maintain a viable program. The coordinator works closely with faculty in developing student and faculty support materials and student evaluation instruments.

The director of Chemeketa Online implements the vision and manages the infrastructure for the online program. Activities include analysis of global community needs and resources, course development, program and course assessment, and research and implementation of new instructional strategies related to online course delivery. The director builds collaborative partnerships with business, industry, education, public agencies, and nonprofit organizations in the delivery of online educational services.

Both full-time and part-time faculty are involved in teaching distance education classes. Faculty report to their instructional department directors, but work closely with the Learning Resource Center director, the Chemeketa Online director, the distance education coordinator, and technical staff.

Key to faculty acceptance is the realization that distance education targets a new audience. Chemeketa's distance education classes do not take students away from current programs, but enhance current programs by bringing in students who would not otherwise be enrolled at the college.

During a time of static or dwindling resources, and when classrooms and parking lots are full, distance education is the means to accommodate new students.

Instructional Strategies

Through participation on committees and task forces, faculty are involved in both planning and oversight of the distance education program. Faculty are responsible for course design, curriculum development, research, and mentoring colleagues. Instructors who teach distance education courses are recruited from instructional departments on campus.

Faculty learn to use distance education technologies via a combination of training strategies, including observation of ongoing classes, mentoring, one-to-one training, group training, and in-house training manuals. Faculty involved in course design are provided release time and/or a stipend depending on each situation. Faculty involved in course development are encouraged to carefully research potential course delivery methods.

Currently, one faculty member is on full-time assignment during the 1995–1996 academic year to develop instructional strategies for online classes. This faculty member is further exploring the possibilities of online instruction in the design of a virtual campus, faculty training, student success, course development, student testing, and program evaluation.

All distance education classes, with the exception of live television, are asynchronous forms of instruction.

Technologies Employed

Prerecorded telecourses are transmitted over public broadcasting and local cable stations in the college district. Videos are made available to students for viewing at local sites, and students have the option of renting videos from a national video rental company.

Live television classes are telecast to college centers; two of the classes are also available directly in students' homes over local cable channels. Students living outside of the district may view the class on videotape. Fire science classes, designed for personnel working in the field, are delivered over local cable to fire stations located in the Chemeketa district. Statewide training employs the use of satellite television, originating from a television studio on the Salem campus. Faculty teaching on live television are mentored by a media specialist who serves as a resource in development and use of the technology.

Three writing classes are offered by correspondence. Correspondence courses include work equivalent to that done in the classroom. Students send assignments to the instructor by mail, and the instructor returns them with detailed comments.

Chemeketa online courses are designed to allow students to schedule class time that is convenient for them. Using a computer and a modem, students participate in discussion groups and send assignments to instructors. Chemeketa Online is accessible via direct dial-in, telnet, or the World Wide Web.

Several general science classes are designed to combine prerecorded telecourses with online instruction. Students view prerecorded telecourse lessons and use Chemeketa Online to send work to their instructor and to engage in discussion groups with classmates. It is possible to obtain a two-year degree solely through the use of online instruction and prerecorded telecourses.

Student Services

Students have access to a toll-free 800 telephone number to call for information on the distance education program. A packet is mailed to each prospective student who requests information. The packet contains a cover letter with instructions on how to enroll at the college, a Chemeketa catalog and schedule of classes, and the necessary forms to have a student admitted to the college and enrolled in a class. Students may register via touch-tone telephone.

A counselor has been designated to provide individual career planning assistance and academic advising to distance education students. This counselor is available to distance education students by calling the 800 number for the distance education office or by electronic mail.

Chemeketa is currently developing online assessment and academic placement tools. Along with career exploration services, a full plan to enhance online student success is coming into place.

Students may access library materials through an online catalog. The online catalog includes the holdings of all public libraries located within the college district. The complete college catalog as well as reciprocal borrowing privileges further link public libraries and academic libraries within the district. Textbooks can be ordered by phone from the college bookstore. Tutoring services are available online; students may make arrangements to have tests proctored at approved sites worldwide.

An online Writing Center, staffed by college writing instructors, makes available instructional expertise and support services to meet the specific writing needs of distance education students. The Writing Center offers flexible writing instruction in all areas of the college curriculum and provides instructional resources to help students write more effectively for school and work. An online Math Center is coming soon.

Student Grading and Program Evaluation

Course content and outcomes for distance education courses are identical to courses taught traditionally. The retention and performance rates for distance education students are equal to, and in many instances greater than, the retention and performance rates for students enrolled in traditional face-to-face classroom instruction. The college is committed to maintaining the highest quality outcomes and standards across all curricula, including distance education.

Unique or Exemplary Practices

Chemeketa Community College is unique in being a pioneer in distance education and in the use of distance education technologies. The college has three degrees available using distance education technologies: the Associate of Arts transfer degree, the Associate of General Studies degree, and the Associate of Applied Science in Fire Protection degree. These degrees are available to students through a combination of alternative deliveries, a mix of on-campus traditional classes and alternative delivery classes, or entirely online.

Chemeketa began delivering classes online in 1991 and currently has over 55 classes developed for online delivery. Online classes are available to students and faculty 24 hours a day, 7 days a week. Access is through direct dial-in or the Internet.

Online classes emphasize student interaction though rich discussion and collaborative work groups. There is no other delivery method that allows each student the opportunity to contribute to the discussion as easily as a Chemeketa Online class. A permanent transcript of all class dialogue and course materials is maintained throughout the entire term and is available to any class participant.

Advantages of the online program for the student include worldwide accessibility and educational opportunities not otherwise available due to time, location, or disability barriers. Other advantages include ongoing interaction with classmates, group work, development of writing and telecommunication skills, and an ability to ruminate before responding.

Faculty also have the advantage of giving thought to a question before responding and appreciate the opportunity to be on the "cutting edge," the ability to set their own schedules, and the ability to accommodate travel, illness, and their personal lives while mentoring a learning group.

Chemeketa students have choices in deciding what is the best instructional delivery plan for them. Many courses are available in several delivery methods, so students can choose which method of instruction they prefer. So while one student may prefer interactive television, another student may prefer an online class. Some students choose to take courses employing a variety of technologies.

Distance education requires a whole new way of thinking about how instruction is delivered, the nature of instruction, and how support services are provided to faculty and students. Obtaining the technology to deliver distance education courses requires funding; the enthusiasm and willing participation of college staff is what will make a distance education program successful.

Chemeketa embraces unique qualities necessary to ensure the success of its distance education program, qualities that make integrating technology into the curriculum a successful venture. Integrating technology into the curriculum to make these opportunities available to students while maintaining high-quality standards is an accomplishment that Chemeketa staff are proud to have achieved.

Donna Carver
Coordinator, Distance Education
Chemeketa Community College
P.O. Box 14007
Salem, OR 97309
(503) 399-5191 or (800)-330-5191; fax: (503)-399-6979
e-mail: donnac@chemek.cc.or.us

Janet King
Director, Chemeketa Online
Chemeketa Community College
P.O. Box 14007
Salem, OR 97309
(503) 399-5191 or (800)-330-5191; fax: (503)-399-6979
e-mail: janet.king@chemek.cc.or.us

Chapter 4

DALLAS COUNTY COMMUNITY COLLEGE DISTRICT
Dallas, Texas

Jacquelyn B. Tulloch

The Dallas County Community College District (DCCCD) serves the metropolitan area of Dallas, Texas, through seven colleges strategically located throughout Dallas County. Together the colleges enroll approximately 50,000 credit and 45,000 noncredit students each long semester.

Distance learning opportunities have existed in the Dallas County Community Colleges for the past 20 years, beginning with the production of the first Dallas telecourse in 1972. At that time, the instructional television department was housed in a temporary trailer and served only a few hundred students. Today, the distance learning program support services are part of the operations of the 28,000 square-foot LeCroy Center for Educational Telecommunications which includes a 1,200 square-foot television studio, computerized editing equipment, a KU-band satellite uplink, and several downlinks. The center not only supports the distance learning program of the Dallas district of colleges but serves as a production and marketing facility for telecourses, teleconferencing, and satellite services. The production unit has produced almost 30 nationally distributed telecourses serving more than 17,000 students in 1,200 colleges each academic year.

Exemplary features of the DCCCD distance learning program include efforts to engage and support learners through the use of multiple technologies, ongoing research and evaluation processes, well-regarded policies concerning faculty remuneration, and the leadership of faculty in program development and delivery. The unique relationship between the production and local implementation units of the DCCCD provides a rich source of information for the improvement of distance learning at home as well as across the nation.

Program Overview

Students Served and Programs Offered

At the present time there are approximately 10,000 enrollments annually in the more than 30 distance learning courses offered each semester through the seven DCCCD colleges. Although these enrollments reflect the same diversity as the student body in general, the majority of students are employed full-time and indicate that distance learning courses are appealing because they respond to the need for flexibility in scheduling due to work, travel, and family commitments.

Coursework offered spans the general transfer curriculum as well as including specific credit and noncredit courses that fill unique needs of the individual DCCCD colleges. In determining program offerings, consideration is given to courses which enable students to complete the A.A.S. degree,

those where low enrollments on each campus may be combined to make a full section, or those for which there is high demand and insufficient on-campus response due to space, number of faculty, or other factors. In response to recent permission from the Texas Higher Education Coordinating Board to offer the A.A.S. degree totally through distance learning courses, the remaining degree fulfilling courses are in development and expected to be in place no later than the spring of 1997. It is noteworthy that more than 80 percent of the courses in the program are offered every semester, making degree completion achievable within a two- to three-year period.

Program Organization

The DCCCD has a somewhat unique distance learning program structure which attempts to blend decentralized enrollment with centralized support and services through the LeCroy Center. This is reflective of the general organizational pattern of the DCCCD as well as the nature of the technologies used in the instructional process.

In general, the colleges are responsible for the broad range of student services such as admission, enrollment, testing, etc. The class schedule and catalog for each college contains the information regarding the program; college personnel are responsible for providing general advising, assistance in course selection, and degree planning. The colleges are also responsible for transcripting all credit hours earned through distance learning courses, and they receive tuition and other funding based on contact hours generated by enrollments.

The Instructional Telecommunications Services department (ITS), housed at the LeCroy Center, is responsible for general program operation. This includes leadership in the process of program planning with the seven colleges, as well as the establishment of broadcast and cable schedules, the development and dissemination of all program information, and publicity. ITS provides general information and ongoing trouble shooting through the operation of specific services for distances learners, such as a hotline, a voicemail system, and the online learning support service provided through the OLLIE computer. ITS is also responsible for the general support of faculty in terms of the production of course materials and research and evaluation activities. Beyond the division of general responsibilities, the colleges and ITS staff have fairly specific and yet somewhat different responsibilities with regard to the three different modes of instructional delivery.

For telecourses, the college academic divisions select, assign, and evaluate course instructors. They also provide assistance in the ordering of textbooks, duplication of course materials, and scheduling of any on-campus course activities. College learning resource centers provide videotapes (and short-term check-out) and are responsible for any other resources identified by faculty for student use. The ITS director at LeCroy selects and works closely with faculty members who serve as "coordinators" for each of the telecourses as well as provide general instructional leadership for the program. Each coordinator is responsible for working with assigned college telecourse instructors across the district to establish course requirements, materials, procedures, and policies. The coordinators draft all instructional materials such as course syllabi, examinations, and newsletters as well as resolve student problems and other issues concerning course content or policies. The coordinators, together with the ITS director, share responsibility for determining research and evaluation processes and the orientation of new telecourse instructors hired by the colleges. In the case of telecourses produced by DCCCD, it is customary for the faculty member who serves as the content specialist for the production of the course to serve as the coordinator when the course is implemented. Each coordinator is remunerated for 60 hours of work with the total contract roughly equivalent to teaching one three-credit-hour course overload. Remuneration for telecourse faculty is the equivalent of one special-service contract or 20 percent of load for each "section" they teach. The number of students defining a full section is based on the "level" of the course. Levels are defined on the basis of both the number and types of interactions with students and the number and types of evaluations graded by faculty. In general, section sizes are similar to those on campus. For example, English composition sections have fewer students than the courses in the area of social sciences.

(Details regarding this policy as well as timelines and other helpful tips regarding the organization and administration of telecourses are detailed in *Successful Practices in Telecourse Implementation,* available from Dallas Telecourses.)

For live televised classes, the colleges and ITS play different roles in the instructional process. Specific courses are proposed to the LeCroy Center by faculty, campus academic leaders, or students. For courses agreed on as suitable offerings by the majority of colleges, a faculty member is selected and contracted directly by the ITS director, usually with advice from a college dean. ITS is responsible for the direct support of the instructor and for most aspects of the instructional process. This includes providing faculty development in the use of the studio, as well as in the design of course materials and presentation techniques. The director, in conjunction with the instructor, determines section size, use of instructional assistants, and support for the production and dissemination of course-related materials.

Faculty developing courses for live televised classes receive the equivalent of one "special service contract" for 60 hours of development activities. This contract is the equivalent of those provided for teaching any three-credit-hour course beyond the defined load, regardless of the method of instruction. Faculty also receive this type of contract for teaching a live televised course, although other arrangements between the ITS and the academic division may be made if special circumstances exist. In the case of "special" credit and noncredit courses offered by single colleges, ITS is responsible only for instructor studio training and technical support for delivery.

Instruction delivered by computer modem is the newest dimension of the program and roles and responsibilities are still in a developmental stage. Currently the college deans and interested faculty at each of the colleges determine the courses which will be offered in this manner, and assign instructors and determine remuneration based on existing guidelines. Other issues such as enrollment limits and student orientations are also the responsibility of the academic division. The ITS provides system server hardware and software, telephone lines, maintenance, and technical support, including a student help desk. In addition, ITS provides faculty development and training in the understanding and use of the system as well as guidance in the conversion of course materials for use on the system. Some of the colleges also provide support for converting course materials, as well as for the development of materials in a multimedia format. Presently any remuneration for faculty developing or converting courses for modem delivery is at the discretion of the college offering the course, with the terms under their control.

Instructional Strategies and Technologies

While currently there are three basic distance learning options—live televised classes; telecourses; and modem-based instruction—a unique feature of the DCCCD program is the rapidly increasing use of multiple technologies in all courses to engage and support the learner. The vast majority of courses in the program may be described as primarily asynchronous instruction, providing for maximum flexibility for students in terms of the time and place of learning.

Telecourses, which form the core of the program, include both print materials as well as video programs and use other asynchronous methods of communication such as voicemail, supplementary audio or video tapes, and increasingly, computer networks. The video programs are shown on local PBS and cable stations, may be viewed at any of the colleges, or leased for the duration of the semester for a nominal charge. Students are required to attend an orientation at the beginning of the semester where they receive an extensive course syllabus and other information viewed as essential for success.

Computer modem courses are the newest part of the DCCCD distance learning effort, and all information is delivered through a specially designed learning environment know as OLLIE (Online Learning, Interaction and Exchange), accessible by modem, telnet, or the DCCCD LAN. There are currently four courses delivered in this manner with several more planned for the future. Students receive lectures, notes, resources, and assignments through the system, participate in group discussions or "forums," and communicate with the instructor or submit completed work through electronic mail. Although students may access OLLIE through DOS with minimum hardware, the Windows-based version is strongly recommended due to its user-friendliness. Students are provided with communications software as well as a multimedia troubleshooting program upon enrollment. One of the special features of this system is its ability to serve as a gateway to the Internet, allowing students to use the world as a source for research, exploration, and learning. Guests may access OLLIE via the World Wide Web at http://ollie.dcccd.edu. While guest access to various screens is limited, a sense of the system is easily garnered on such a visit.

Live televised classes are the only predominately synchronous form of instruction offered in the DCCCD distance learning program. Classes originate at an instructor studio at the LeCroy Center, and may be delivered over the ITFS system, by satellite downlink to sites equipped to receive the signal, or into homes over the channels of local cable companies. Students are required to view the classes at the time of broadcast, although they may do this from a variety of locations at a distance from the instructor. Students participate and interact with the instructor during class time through telephone lines from home or through press-to-talk microphones from ITFS or satellite downlink sites. An audio bridge permits a number of students to participate simultaneously. The instructor studio is equipped with three cameras, a multimedia computer with CD-ROM, extensive software for graphics and Internet access, as well as a VCR and a videodisc player. While technical support is always nearby and broadcasts are continuously monitored for problems, the studio is operated solely by the instructor. Course instructors are responsible for the preparation and content of all instruction and are assisted in converting their materials for use on live television, using the technologies available in the studio.

Faculty developing courses for live televised classes receive compensation for 60 hours of development work, which is the equivalent of a contract for teaching one three-credit-hour course beyond the defined load. They also receive the standard "special service contract" for teaching the course. In these live classes, when enrollments exceed what is reasonable, the faculty member is assisted by an instructional associate who helps with telephone calls, grading, and other duties.

Technologies Employed

Various ancillary technologies are used by different instructors in telecourses, computer modem courses, and in the live televised classes. While many telecourse faculty still provide on-campus orientations, discussion groups, test reviews, and are available for private appointments in person, an increasing number conduct these and other interactions with students using various forms of technologies that provide greater flexibility. Voicemail, a relatively inexpensive and highly accessible form of technology, is used for private messaging for both students and faculty as well as for group announcements and general information. In the teaching of English composition and Spanish, it is used as a more integral part of instruction, providing an alternative mode for student collaboration and oral assignments. Audio and/or videotapes are commonly used to provide orientations, test review information, or particularly troublesome course concepts. Students may either check out such tapes at the colleges or "dub" them for later use. An increasing number of faculty are using the online computer system, OLLIE, as an alternative

for communicating for students with access to PCs with modems. OLLIE features both private e-mail as well as the discussion forums related to course content. Other options used by instructors include the use of an audioconferencing system with 24 lines for discussion groups, audio "office hours," and test review sessions. While this form of technology is time-bound, students respond positively to being able to participate from any location by telephone. Faculty and students in live televised classes also make use of voice, e-mail, regular mail, and fax for information exchange, feedback, and course assignments.

Student Grading and Program Evaluation

Faculty are responsible for all processes related to the evaluation of student learning and, while courses vary in terms of requirements, all distance learning courses require written work in the form of assignments, essays, research papers, or tests. In some courses, field activities, case problems, and special projects are also a part of measuring student progress. Students receive both quantitative as well as written feedback on all tests and assignments.

The DCCCD program includes regular opportunities to evaluate program effectiveness. Students complete evaluations at midsemester as well as at the end of the course. In live televised classes, the midsemester "pulse check" is informal and open-ended in design as students and instructor are in relatively constant contact. The midsemester survey for telecourse students is much more detailed and designed to provide feedback to college instructors on items such as the clarity and value of orientation, accessibility of instructors, and self-estimates of progress or need for assistance. At the conclusion of the semester, all distance learning students complete surveys related to the course which focus on the quality of materials and instructional process as well as the support services provided.

Faculty meet each semester to review a variety of information such as enrollment and grade distribution statistics, test item analyses, and student evaluations. This information, in combination with personal observations, is used to make changes in content, requirements, policies, and procedures. In addition, relevant evaluative information is distributed to all departments providing services and support, such as testing centers and educational resource centers. The information collected through the surveys provides a profile of the distance learners in the DCCCD and enables the LeCroy Center and instructional faculty and staff to determine future courses and services.

Unique or Exemplary Practices

One of the truly unique features of the distance learning program in the DCCCD is the symbiotic relationship between the national production and distribution processes and the direct delivery and support of courses within the college district. Faculty, students, and administrators of the program are an important source of feedback, facilitating improvements in the quality of telecourse productions as well as directing the focus of future projects.

From its inception more than 20 years ago, the telecourse design and production unit has been driven by the needs of students. While input is gathered from the 1,200 colleges and universities who lease the college's products, DCCCD students continue to serve as a microcosm of the national audience, and are the most direct source of input and feedback for the structure and content of video programs, print materials, and support services. For example, the student evaluation process described elsewhere in this chapter was designed and is used, in part, to provide detailed feedback regarding telecourse video and print materials. This information is integrated into the revision process for each specific course as well as into the overall strategic planning process.

At the same time, students provide critical input on the value of specific course implementation strategies and services. This information not only helps to improve the local program but often leads to the development of new products. One such example is "The Emerging Learner," a nationally marketed video series that serves as a generic introduction to distance learning and the skills necessary for success, but the series was the net result of much less polished local efforts to respond to the need for improved study skills and retention in distance learning courses.

Just as student and faculty feedback in Dallas improves telecourses and the support services necessary for student success, the links with other colleges and universities through the production and marketing units of the center are a source of information about innovations and successful practices across the country. This information frequently leads to improvements in the local program and is, in turn, shared with others through the telecourse faculty manuals or through publications such as the recent monograph, *Successful Practices in Telecourse Implementation.*

In these cases, as in many others not cited here, because the center is both a production house as well as a local service provider, it is able to identify common needs, consolidate resources, and share costs for improving distance learning programs not only for local students but for those at colleges across the country.

Jacquelyn B. Tulloch
Executive Dean, Distance Education
LeCroy Center for Educational Telecommunications
7576 Walnut Street
Dallas, TX 75243
(972) 669-6408; fax: (972) 669-6409
e-mail: jackiet@dcccd.edu
URL: http://lecroy.dcccd.edu

Chapter 5

FLORIDA COMMUNITY COLLEGE AT JACKSONVILLE
Jacksonville, Florida

Eleanor L. Minich

Florida Community College at Jacksonville (FCCJ) is a public, two-year comprehensive community college enrolling over 94,000 students annually in a variety of academic, training, and enrichment courses and programs. FCCJ is the second largest community college in the state and the tenth largest in the nation.

Starting in 1980 with two telecourses on educational access cable television, the distance education program at FCCJ now includes over 35 credit and continuing education telecourses, 160 teleconferences annually, community forums on public television, award-winning educational and informational television series, pilot projects, and technological innovations.

In 1987, the Open Campus was established to better serve nontraditional populations with college-credit and continuing education courses and activities. Distance education is an integral part of the mission of Open Campus, which provides leadership and management for FCCJ's distance learning activities.

Program Overview

Students Served and Programs Offered

Distance education at FCCJ strongly supports the college's institutional mission of excellent teaching, meaningful learning, and student success. FCCJ serves college-credit students seeking an associate's degree, local community members interested in continuing education and personal or professional development opportunities, regional and state agencies requiring training or curriculum development, and a national audience of educational institutions seeking video-based instructional materials.

Telecourse students are the largest and most significant group of distance learners at FCCJ. With over 6,000 students enrolled in 35 college-credit telecourses each year, FCCJ's distance learning program is the largest in the state. Telecourse offerings include courses in accounting, algebra, American history, anthropology, biology, business law, chemistry, computer science, economics, English, French, humanities, literature, management, marketing, political science, psychology, religion, sales, sociology, and statistics.

Twenty-three telecourses fulfill the general education or foreign language requirements for the associate in arts degree, and an additional 11 telecourses are either degree electives or course prerequisites. All degree requirements are available though televised instruction, with only two exceptions: a three-credit-hour speech class and a one-credit-hour laboratory science class.

Academic Year	Courses Offered	Students Served	FTE
1989–90	26	3,976	298.2
1990–91	28	4,698	352.3
1991–92	30	5,522	414.2
1992–93	30	5,255	394.1
1993–94	32	5,407	405.5
1994–95	34	6,012	450.9

Figure 5-1

Distance learning has steadily attracted an increasing student audience at FCCJ. As indicated in Figure 5-1, the number of college-credit students studying via telecourse increased by 51 percent between 1990 and 1995.

FCCJ regularly surveys its telecourse students to determine who enrolls in telecourses, why they chose distance learning, and how the telecourse program can be improved to better meet student needs.

In winter term 1995, the average telecourse student was white (76 percent), female (69 percent), approximately 31 years old, and seeking an associate in arts degree (61 percent) while employed outside the home (78 percent). Most telecourse students were enrolling at FCCJ for at least the fourth time (78 percent) and receiving some form of financial aid (54 percent).

Telecourse students have at least one VCR (95 percent), at least two televisions (80 percent), and have personal access to a computer at home or at work (74 percent). Only 27 percent of these students viewed telecourse lessons during regularly scheduled cablecasts, with 54 percent videotaping the lessons for more convenient viewing at a later time, 23 percent visiting a campus learning resource center to view taped lessons, and 3 percent renting the tapes from a private distributor for use on a home VCR.

Why do students enroll in telecourses at FCCJ? Here are two typical student comments from a recent survey: "This program allows me more time for my family obligations..." and "I enjoy the convenience of furthering my education and my career at the same time. Telecourses provide the flexibility to do this."

These student comments clearly illustrate the two primary motivations for telecourse enrollment: personal responsibilities and professional commitments. FCCJ's distance learners are working adults with busy personal schedules, attracted by the flexibility and convenience of distance education.

Interestingly, distance education is not the first choice of all telecourse students. Nearly 20 percent of all telecourse students—about 1,200 annually—enrolled as an alternative to full or canceled campus-based classes. Thus, distance education provides FCCJ with a mechanism for serving students who might otherwise have been turned away, and is a complementary component to traditional campus-based instruction.

While it is clear that distance education may be the most convenient and flexible educational opportunity for adults with career and personal commitments, it is not the only avenue for most of FCCJ's telecourse students. Students who study exclusively via telecourses are a minority. Nearly 60 percent of all telecourse students are concurrently enrolled on campus, discrediting the belief that nontraditional programs are "stealing" students from more traditional programs of study. At FCCJ, distance education and traditional classroom-based programs are sharing students rather than competing for them.

Finally, it is not surprising that most of FCCJ telecourse students enroll in telecourses for the same reasons traditional students enroll in campus-based courses: to fulfill degree requirements. Fall 1994 survey results indicate that 78 percent of telecourse students enrolled to fulfill a degree requirement with another 16 percent enrolling to complete an elective course for a degree program. Nontraditional community college students are no less practical than on-campus students.

College-credit students have another distance learning option besides telecourses at FCCJ. Computer-based courses are offered through FCCJ's electronic bulletin board service. Distance learners are mailed a diskette with FirstClass™ bulletin board software, a welcome letter from the instructor, and an instruction sheet for installation of the software. The software (available for Windows and Macintosh systems) is free and the connection to the bulletin board is a local telephone call. Students access course materials, participate in discussions, and post written assignments to the course instructor.

In addition to the credit students served by FCCJ, a smaller, but no less important audience served by distance learning includes local community members interested in professional development, personal enrichment, and informational updates. This audience is served through FCCJ's televised forums, teleconferences, and video productions.

FCCJ's Special Projects Office regularly produces televised community forums in cooperation with the local PBS television affiliate. For the past four years, FCCJ has produced approximately six forums each year on topics such as crime, education, health care, and government. Videotaped before a live studio audience for later broadcast and focused on an important community issue, each forum is a moderated discussion between an audience of community residents and a panel of prominent experts. One of these forums, "A Line in the Sand: The Mideast Crisis," won the 1991 Florida Association of Community Colleges Community Service Project of the Year Award.

FCCJ also serves the residents of Northeast Florida via teleconferencing. FCCJ's Open Campus downlinks over 150 teleconferences annually, offering a wide range of environmental, educational, professional, and business topics of interest to corporations, small businesses, nonprofit organizations, governmental agencies, and educational institutions. FCCJ is also the designated downlink site in Northeast Florida for the statewide satellite teleconferencing network, SUNSTAR. Numerous programs are offered throughout the year including press conferences, public forums, legislative updates, and continuing education.

In addition to these teleconference downlinks, FCCJ has also produced and uplinked teleconferences. For example, FCCJ received a contract from the state of Florida to produce, uplink, and distribute via satellite timely information on new drug and alcohol legislation. This teleconference provided training to 500 state employees at 17 sites throughout the state. Edited videotapes of this teleconference serve as the basis for ongoing training on this legislation.

On a regional level, FCCJ is a leading partner in the Northeast Florida Distance Learning Consortium, representing educational partners from K-12, community college, university, cable and public television, and other educational agencies. This consortium received a grant from the Florida State Board of Regents to develop a conflict resolution curriculum targeting middle school students and their parents, teachers, and staff. In support of this grant, FCCJ is completing production of the video components for "A Distance Learning Project in Conflict Resolution."

Finally, FCCJ is a nationally recognized producer of telecourses and video series, reaching a wide market across the United States and Canada. *Read, Write, Research*, an English composition telecourse produced by FCCJ, is currently in use by 31 colleges and five consortia and enrolled over 2,500 college-credit students last year. FCCJ's production list also includes the series *Author, Author!*, *Writer to Writer*, *Teaching, Learning, Technology*, and *Innovative Teaching and Learning*. All of these series are in national distribution by PBS/Adult Learning Service.

Program Organization

Distance education at FCCJ is a collaborative effort by the assistant instructional dean, the telecourse office, and the television production unit.

Reporting directly to the president of Open Campus, the assistant dean supervises several large college-credit programs: telecourses and online courses; Weekend College and an accelerated weekend program; and all military education offered at the three U.S. Navy installations in the Jacksonville area. In support of the telecourse program, the assistant dean negotiates telecourse licenses, oversees budget and finances, monitors academic quality, previews new telecourses, and evaluates program effectiveness. The assistant dean also serves in a leadership role on the national Executive Board of the Instructional Telecommunications Council, an AACC affiliate, and the Florida Community College Television Consortium, a statewide consortium representing the distance learning interests of all 28 Florida community colleges. Active participation in state and national distance learning organizations provides FCCJ with access to information on recent government legislation, technological developments affecting distance education, and trends in higher education. The assistant dean also manages the marketing of FCCJ telecourse productions.

Day-to-day operation of the telecourse program is the responsibility of a program coordinator who reports directly to the assistant dean. The program coordinator plans and selects the telecourse offerings each term, develops the television schedule, recruits and trains faculty, manages the development and distribution of course materials, coordinates testing activities, acts as liaison with the college bookstores and learning resource centers, and markets and promotes telecourses. The telecourse program coordinator position is key to the success of distance education.

All technical aspects of telecourse production and delivery, including liaison with cable television operators, programming machines, licensure application and procedures, equipment maintenance, and assurance of broadcast quality are the responsibility of the television production department. Cablecasting of FCCJ telecourses originates in the Open Campus television studio, where videotaped lessons are transmitted via ITFS for telecasting over educational access cable television in a two-county area of Northeast Florida. FCCJ's television producer and engineer preview telecourse video materials and approve their technical quality before telelessons are aired.

Faculty are responsible for the academic and instructional integrity of distance education at FCCJ, and hold the same academic and professional qualifications as their colleagues teaching the same discipline on campus. Of the 42 telecourse faculty in fall term 1995, 88 percent are full-time faculty and 12 percent are adjunct faculty. All faculty hold a minimum of an earned master's degree, with 35 percent of all telecourses taught by faculty holding the doctoral degree. Full-time faculty from all five FCCJ campuses teach telecourses. To involve as many interested faculty as possible, telecourse teaching assignments are made on a rotating basis, with adjunct faculty assigned to telecourse instruction when full-time faculty are unavailable.

FCCJ faculty teach telecourses as part of their regular workload or as an overload. Compensation is based on the faculty member's educational qualifications and the number of students enrolled in the telecourse. Overloads are awarded when telecourse class sizes exceed preset enrollment allocations. These allocations are based on the amount of written work required of students. Currently, the telecourse allocation for English composition is 30 students, while the allocation for humanities, accounting, foreign languages, economics, computer science, and certain social science courses is 45. All other telecourses are allocated at 60 students.

Faculty teaching telecourses enrolling fewer students than the allocation are guaranteed to receive at least three or four points towards a 15-point-per-term teaching load. Telecourses with enrollment below 20 are usually canceled. Where enrollment exceeds allocation, faculty compensation is increased proportionally.

Faculty teaching telecourses are required to conduct an on-campus orientation for students and administer examinations on campus. Faculty communicate regularly with students by telephone and mail, answering questions, commenting on tests and homework assignments, and explaining other course requirements. Instructors develop a syllabus which includes telelesson and examination schedules, textbook information, assignments, and other information the instructor deems necessary. All written assignments and examinations are mailed directly to the instructor for evaluation, grading, and feedback to students.

College funds are earmarked for operation of the telecourse program with no support from grant sources. An operational budget covers staff salaries, telecourse licenses fees, educational and office materials, and professional development activities. Discipline-specific instructional budgets cover adjunct faculty salaries, instructional materials, and faculty professional development. A $5 fee is collected each time a student enrolls in a telecourse, with the resulting revenues deposited into a telecourse program contingency fund.

Other FCCJ distance education projects are grant funded, operated on a contractual basis with an outside organization, or are self-supporting activities. Television production is funded by a separate operational budget.

FCCJ supports and rewards faculty involvement with technology. For the past seven years, the college has sponsored an Annual National Conference on Teaching, Learning, and Technology. Over 450 participants attended the sixth annual conference held in Jacksonville in April 1995, sharing innovative ideas and practical applications of instructional technology to further student learning. Video programs based on the conference are distributed nationally.

FCCJ's Center for the Advancement of Teaching and Learning sponsors faculty professional development opportunities and awards minigrants to faculty interested in developing and piloting multimedia course components. The FCCJ Innovative Faculty Technology Award is presented annually to a faculty member who has distinguished him or herself in the development or application of instructional technology.

Instructional Strategies

Distance education at FCCJ is designed to provide nontraditional students with learning opportunities equivalent in academic content, objectives, and outcomes to traditional methods of learning. The technology of distance learning delivery provides flexibility and convenience to working adults returning to college, while the academic quality, learning objectives, and course requirements meet accreditation standards.

Faculty are responsible for the academic integrity of telecourses and ensure that telecourses are the equivalent of the same academic courses taught on campus. All learning goals and objectives, academic content and approaches, academic level, evaluation measures, and textbooks are equivalent to on-campus offerings. The technological manner in which instruction is delivered to distance learners is the only substantial difference between nontraditional and traditional instruction.

Of the 35 telecourses currently used at FCCJ, the majority (86 percent) are licensed from major telecourse producers and the remainder (15 percent) are FCCJ productions. Prior to adopting any telecourse, the video component is first evaluated by the television producer and/or engineer to assure that the technical quality of the video meets or exceeds acceptable broadcast standards. If video standards are not met, the telecourse is not considered by the faculty for adoption.

After technical approval, faculty members with the appropriate academic background review the preview package of videotaped and print components to determine the comparability of academic objectives, content, and level with existing college courses, evaluate the overall instructional approach, and decide if any adaptation is necessary before offering the telecourse. Faculty approval is necessary before the adoption of any telecourse.

Faculty members then design the course components, including course syllabus, selection of texts, broadcast sequence of lessons, type and number of required written assignments and examinations. They also develop a detailed schedule for the telecourse, assigning specific text materials to be read, lessons to be viewed, assignments to be completed and mailed, and examinations to be taken during each week of the telecourse.

Telecourse students work independently of their fellow telecourse students—after the initial orientation session at the start of the term, telecourse students rarely have contact with other students in their telecourse. Faculty are available to students via telephone conferences. On-campus meetings between telecourse students and faculty may be scheduled but are infrequent, since telecourse students are normally unable to come to campus because of personal schedules and obligations.

All FCCJ's online courses are custom designed by faculty. Unlike telecourses, there are currently no preproduced, commercially available computer-based courses for preview and possible adoption. Faculty are responsible for the academic integrity, content and design of computer-based instruction.

While computer-based instruction may appear on the surface to be less personal than face-to-face teaching and learning, online instruction has promoted more regular and frequent exchanges between students and faculty. Students also appear to be more willing to engage in lively discussions of controversial topics online, whereas in the classroom they may have been more reluctant to voice an unpopular opinion or viewpoint.

Students are subject to the same admission policies, placement testing requirements, and course prerequisites whether they enroll in a course delivered in the classroom or via technology. All students have access to touch-tone telephone registration during regularly scheduled college registration periods.

Distance learning course schedules are scheduled during the regular college terms: fall (August–December, 15 weeks), winter (January–May, 15 weeks), spring (May–June, 6 weeks), cross term (May–August, 12 weeks), and summer (July–August, 6 weeks). Distance learning courses, however, more readily accommodate late registrations since telecourse lessons are available on videotape in all campus learning resource centers, and all online courses post lectures, assignments, and syllabus on the electronic bulletin board.

There is a special late registration period for telecourses and online courses since students may work at their own pace and easily make up missed lessons.

Other telecommunications-based programs at FCCJ—teleconferences, televised public forums, and television productions—are noncredit continuing education opportunities, and therefore do not involve the enrollment of participants as FCCJ students.

Technologies Employed

FCCJ uses a variety of instructional technologies to facilitate student learning at a distance, including Instructional Television Fixed Service (ITFS), microwave and satellite technologies, cable and public television broadcasting, T-1 and fiber-optic lines, voicemail, a computer bulletin board, the Internet, and videotape production and duplication. The target audience, program content, and objectives determine the technology used.

Faculty and telecourse students interact regularly via telephone, voicemail, mail, and in person. Future plans include the establishment of voicemail for each registered telecourse student to promote further interaction. As mentioned previously, faculty teaching online interact with students via the college's electronic bulletin board service, offered via FirstClass™ software.

While satellite technology is the basis of all teleconferencing activities at FCCJ, interaction in teleconferences is conducted via telephone. Other pilot projects have employed two-way audio and video communication between faculty and students via either T-1 lines or compressed video satellite systems.

To address the choices presented by the speed and frequency of technological change and the variety of delivery systems on the market, FCCJ has established a technology planning team, tasked with the design and development of a comprehensive strategic technology plan to integrate voice, video, and data for implementation collegewide. To meet this ambitious goal, a Request for Proposal was issued, responses carefully evaluated, and a consulting firm selected. As this chapter is written, consultants have begun work on this technology plan.

Student access to technology is another important issue. While 74 percent of telecourse students have personal access to computers either at work or at home, the majority of these computers have no modem, no communications software, and no access to any online services. Equal access to technology for all students must be incorporated into FCCJ's technology plan.

Student Services

All students are subject to the same admission policies, placement testing requirements, and course prerequisites whether they enroll in a course delivered in the classroom or via technology. Furthermore, distance learners have equal access to student services as on-campus students.

Admissions of distance learners are handled primarily through the mail, with transcripts of transfer credits transmitted electronically. Student records for distance learners are identical in form and content to records maintained for on-campus students. There is no differentiation on transcripts between courses taught on campus or via technology.

Students may register for college-credit courses, add or drop classes, designate alternate classes if their first choices classes are already full, and pay tuition and fees with a credit card via touch-tone telephone. Thirty-two telephone lines are available during peak registration periods. Students may also choose to remit payment via regular mail.

Distance learners have the same access to learning resources and support as on-campus students. Each campus has a librarian to serve its students. Even though Open Campus does not have its own library collection, a fully qualified librarian has been assigned to the Open Campus to assist students who study via distance learning. This librarian conducts special library orientations for distance learners, and assists students conducting research.

Learning resource centers are open days, evenings, and weekends to accommodate a variety of student schedules. The Library Information Network for Interlibrary Loan (LINCC) allows students to electronically review the catalogs of library collections at all Florida community colleges, and to access pertinent information through interlibrary loan. Distance learners also have access to a variety of learning support, including tutorial help at all campuses and centers.

The telecourse packet, automatically mailed to students when they enroll in telecourses, includes the course syllabus; faculty contact information; homework, testing, and broadcast schedules; tape rental and textbook information; and college policies and administrative procedures for telecourses. Students enrolled in computer-based courses can access course information online, including the syllabus, assignments, testing and grading information, and faculty contact information.

Students may order instructional materials from any campus bookstore via telephone or fax for direct shipment to the student's home or for campus pickup at a later date. Textbooks, software, audiotapes, study guides, and other course materials may be obtained through this delivery service. Students also have the option of renting telecourse tapes from a private distribution house, which will ship the video series to the student's home. Free software to access FCCJ's electronic bulletin board is mailed to all registered students, who also have the option of downloading the software.

The telecourse office is the primary provider of administrative and procedural advice to distance learners. Information on college policies, deadlines, and procedures is included in the telecourse syllabus mailed to the student's home. In addition, information screens containing orientation and testing dates and sites, and other time-sensitive telecourse information are regularly and frequently cablecast between programs.

Open Campus also has a telephone line dedicated to providing prerecorded telecourse updates 24 hours a day. Student questions or concerns that require special attention are referred to the assistant dean or appropriate college office.

Open Campus is equipped with a TDD for communication with disabled students, and all telecourse staff are trained in its

use. In addition, programs produced at the college are closed captioned for the hearing-impaired. When closed captioning is not available, telelesson transcripts are made available to students requesting this accommodation. FCCJ's Disabled Student Services Center is always available to provide necessary services and accommodations to distance learners with special needs, including note-takers, interpreters, readers, and other assistance to facilitate student access and success.

FCCJ is currently negotiating an articulation agreement with a four-year university to give students who have earned a two-year associate's degree from FCCJ the option of completing a bachelor's degree via distance learning. Designed specifically for working adults, distance learners will be able to complete a four-year degree regardless of location, professional obligations, or personal time constraints.

Student Grading and Program Evaluation

Faculty members evaluate student progress through written assignments and examinations, provide feedback directly to students, and assign grades. Written assignments may include term papers, research projects, business plans, textbook exercises, book reports, or other assignments. Faculty-developed written examinations range from essay to multiple-choice questions. Faculty have the responsibility and authority to determine what assignments and examinations will be required of students.

FCCJ has designed a convenient, secure testing service to accommodate distance learners throughout Jacksonville. Students may choose to take examinations on campus with the instructor or at one of the alternate testing locations administered by the telecourse office. Alternate testing is available at four locations in two counties in the evenings and on weekends, and students are required to present two forms of personal identification, one of which must be a picture I.D., before admission to the testing room.

Coordination of the testing function is a major undertaking by the telecourse office, since the average telecourse requires three to four written examinations of each registered student. In the 1996 fall term alone, approximately 3,000 examinations were administered by this testing service.

With grading standards and policies clearly stated in course syllabi, faculty are strongly encouraged to grade in the same manner normally employed for on-campus courses. Many faculty members use the same assignments, examinations, grading techniques, and scale that they use on campus. The only college personnel with the authority to award or change grades are the faculty.

The distance education program at FCCJ is continuously improved through feedback from faculty, student, and staff evaluations. Each term, students evaluate the quality of service provided by staff and faculty, and rate the components and design of telecourses. Student evaluations are anonymous and conducted after final grades have been assigned. Written comments are encouraged. This system of student course evaluations was recently automated to allow a more thorough analysis of the data collected.

Students who register and subsequently withdraw from distance education courses are also surveyed each term to determine the reason for their withdrawals. These surveys are also anonymous, with written comments encouraged. The withdrawal survey has been particularly helpful in explaining the higher rates of withdrawal from telecourses as compared to classroom-based courses. Withdrawal surveys consistently indicate that distance learners withdraw from telecourses for the same reasons for which they originally registered: busy personal schedules and personal obligations.

For example, in the 1995 winter term, 69 percent of students who withdrew from telecourses stated that their withdrawals were due to personal reasons, with many citing changes in job schedules, required business travel, or family obligations. The majority of these students admitted that they had never contacted the instructor (58 percent), never contacted the telecourse office (66 percent), never submitted required assignments (52 percent), and never took an examination (57 percent). Yet most of these students (55 percent) indicated that they intended to enroll in telecourses again, and another 20 percent said they would consider enrolling in telecourses in the future.

Finally, grade distributions are analyzed and compared to student achievement in the same courses offered on campus, and faculty input is regularly solicited by program staff, who note problems to be solved or innovations to be implemented.

Improvements in distance education have resulted from the careful analysis of faculty, student, and staff feedback. Courses and testing sites have been added, broadcast schedules adjusted, course materials revised, examinations rewritten, brochures redesigned, and opportunities identified. Most of the statistical information included in this chapter was gathered from student surveys.

Unique or Exemplary Practices

From 1991 to 1993, FCCJ participated in a pilot project funded by a special appropriation in the U.S. Department of Defense budget. The purpose of this project was to determine the feasibility of community colleges reconfiguring site-based military occupational specialty (MOS) training and then delivering this reconfigured curriculum via video teletraining

to multiple sites in Florida.

FCCJ used the U.S. Army's teletraining network, "TNet," a two-way compressed video satellite communications system as its delivery system. Training originated in Jacksonville at FCCJ and was then transmitted via the TNet system to receive sites at Valencia Community College and St. Petersburg Junior College. An additional receive site was also established at FCCJ to allow project evaluators the opportunity to observe and assess training activities at the origination and receive sites in a single visit.

FCCJ designed, developed, and delivered this distance learning curriculum using community college faculty and military subject matter experts to train Army reservists and the National Guard. FCCJ also collaborated with the University of Central Florida, Valencia Community College, and St. Petersburg Junior College to reconfigure the MOS training curriculum used by the Army in its traditional site-based training. The resulting teletraining curriculum satisfied the requirements of both MOS and college-credit courses—that is, military service members participating in the teletraining pilot could earn both MOS certification and college credit for the same course of study.

The pilot program produced a distance learning curriculum and an instructional model, as well as print and video materials for the U.S. Department of Defense. It also developed a cadre of community college faculty and staff trained in state-of-the-art interactive video technology, provided military service members with MOS certification and some college credit, and received a positive evaluation by the Institute for Simulation and Training at the University of Central Florida.

Eleanor L. Minich
Assistant Instructional Dean, Open Campus
Florida Community College at Jacksonville
101 West State Street, Room A-1181
Jacksonville, Florida 32202
(904) 633-8359; fax: (904) 633-8435
e-mail: eminich@fccjvm.fccj.cc.fl.us

Chapter 6

GENESEE COMMUNITY COLLEGE
Batavia, New York

Robert G. Knipe

At Genesee Community College, distance learning is an asynchronous mix of standard telecourses adapted for greater interaction and improved access to campus resources by the distant student, and locally produced courses using print, audio, video, and computer networks. Both approaches are backed by strong advising, required orientation, and student and faculty support components which result in high faculty participation and a student on-time course completion rate in the 80 percent range.

Genesee is a 3,200 FTE comprehensive community college serving four counties in rural Western New York State with a population of about a quarter million primarily living in towns of 18,000 or fewer. The economic base is devoted to agriculture and small manufacturing; many residents commute to urban areas to the east (Rochester) and west (Buffalo). The college opened its doors in 1967, and in 1972 moved to a new single-building campus two miles outside Batavia.

Ninety-five percent of the student population commutes. Demographics reveal an average student age of just under 30. Growth is increasingly from the working adult student population. To this end, the college began opening fully staffed campus centers of six to ten classrooms each in towns 25 to 50 miles distant from the main campus. These centers have seen double-to-triple-digit annual growth since the first of four opened in 1991.

Distance learning offerings have also grown considerably since the first telecourses were leased in 1987. The various courses and programs—including modified telecourses in five correctional facilities—were administratively consolidated in 1990 to report to one rather than the previous three administrators.

In 1991, the college was awarded a federal Title III grant to enhance interaction and resource access in distance learning courses. The combination of new markets, rapid growth in enrollment, opening of campus centers, consolidation of distance learning efforts, and external funding matched an institutional commitment to providing comparable access to resources for distance learning students.

A critical element in the implementation of distance learning at Genesee was the strong support of appropriate instructional technology. GCC pioneered the use of touch-screen student information terminals and had one of the first voicemail systems in the region to feature student accounts. Its six main-campus and six off-campus computer labs are networked with the college's VAX system, and registered students are issued e-mail accounts. Seventy percent of full-time faculty have computers in their offices. Internet access and training are provided, and student

access is being explored.

The GCC library was automated in 1984, added a librarian assigned half-time to off-campus services in 1992, and now supports an automated catalog, a full-text online periodical database, Internet access to nine databases, reference services, and intra- and interlibrary loan at all campus locations.

The external technology environment includes a cable television provider with a service "footprint" approximating the college's service area; several telephone utilities with relatively little fiber-optic backbone in place; and severe winter weather and hilly terrain making line-of-sight transmission media an expensive proposition.

Given this institutional culture and technology environment, it was an easy decision to orient distance learning efforts around five guiding principles: 1) focus on qualitative issues, and the numbers will follow; 2) use appropriate and supportable technology, not fearing default to low-tech solutions; 3) ensure distance learning courses remain an outgrowth of campus curricular core, and ownership remains with mainstream faculty; 4) build in significant opportunity for instructor-student and student-student interaction; and 5) remain centered on student needs.

Program Overview

Students Served

Genesee currently serves a bimodal population. Full-time, main-campus day students are traditionally college age: more than 70 percent are under 25. Part-time, off-campus, evening and distance learning students fit a different profile also familiar to community colleges: modal age is between 29 and 45; 70 percent are female; and 70 percent work outside the home. The latter group—the college's most underserved population and a large potential growth market—is perceived as needing asynchronous credit course opportunities.

Marketing is done primarily through course bulletins bulk-mailed to 90,000-plus households three times annually, with distance learning courses featured in a one-and-a-half-page spread. Drive-time radio spots, newspaper, and Pennysaver ads are also used, and the program has been the topic of several area newspaper features. Brochures, detailed lists of course requirements and resources, and other materials are available three to five months in advance of the each semester at all campus locations and in the communities served. Main-campus-based students make up 25 to 30 percent of distance learning course enrollments, although this is not the target market.

Programs Offered

From four standard telecourses per semester in 1989, Genesee now offers 18 to 22 courses per semester, across the curriculum. Current courses represent nearly all transfer and many career/vocational divisions: accounting, business, biology, economics, health, history, human services, humanities and literature, math, office technology, physics, psychology, and sociology. Seventy percent are leased courses adapted from the offerings of major telecourse providers. Thirty percent are homegrown courses, either evolved from courses leased earlier or developed entirely by GCC faculty and staff.

GCC courses available via distance learning now cover a broad enough range of general education and elective courses that it is possible to complete General Studies associate's degree requirements in this manner. But distance learning courses are not a formal stand-alone degree option; they are part of a broad range of options for working adult students who in most cases complete a mix of courses including distance learning, off-campus, and on-campus conventional courses. Technically, GCC meets the criteria for "Going The Distance" participation. The college, however, has no immediate plans to advertise a complete degree via distance learning, nor does it use PBS-affiliate stations for telecourse program dissemination.

Program Organization

Responsibility for course content, objectives and exit competencies, quality control, curriculum, and program "fit" rests with academic departments. Genesee does not have a separate department of distance learning or continuing education; English 01 "belongs" to the English department and Humanities division, no matter where or how taught. The associate dean supervising the academic or career area and the associate dean for Learning Resources communicate closely about course offerings and faculty assignments.

Course planning is done collaboratively by the associate deans of academic divisions, Off-Campus Credit Instruction, and Learning Resources. Each of the four campus centers is administered by an assistant dean, who is also very active in the process of course planning.

Learning Resources provides overall vision and coordinates record-keeping and assessment. Technology support is coordinated through Learning Resources, along with media, library, and academic support services.

Faculty look to Learning Resources staff for specific direction and support. Overall load assignments and evaluations are the responsibility of the academic division deans. Over 90 percent of distance learning faculty are full-time, and distance learning courses fit within a normal five-course load. Part-time instructors are paid $1,467 to $1,617 per three-credit course, depending on seniority. Full-time faculty teaching on overload status are paid at part-time rates. During the 1991–94 Title III project, participating faculty were also paid a one-time $1,000 stipend for course development, and given a computer, software, and network access. (The computer proved to be the more highly valued perk.) No release time or stipends are currently given for new

course development. Still, in the 1994–95 academic year, eight new faculty came forward with proposals which have been or are planned to be offered.

Maximum section sizes for distance learning courses vary between 24 and 40. Minimum size is 15. Few are canceled for low enrollment, and half or more each semester have students on a waiting list. Mean section size is typically 27 to 29, counted after fourth-week drops.

No single Genesee Community College employee exclusively supports distance learning full-time. Professional staff time allocations vary: Learning Resources, Media Services, off-campus/reference librarians, and Academic Computing staff devote between 10 and 60 percent of their time to support of distance learning. During the 1991–94 Title III grant period, 1.5 FTE staff assisted in materials development, faculty training, establishment of procedures, and general support of distance learning. Since 1994, all grant-supported functions have been institutionalized and absorbed by college-funded staff.

Since 70 percent of distance learning students are located away from the main campus, operational support of these students falls heavily on staff at campus centers. These centers are small, and one-stop service is a guiding mindset. A weekday-evening team of one part-time administrative assistant and a secretary might, for example, oversee eight conventional classes and a full computer lab in the building, advise new or prospective adult students, channel financial aid papers, assist network log-ins, check out tapes to distance learning students, proctor exams, schedule students with tutors, send faxes, help faculty with the copier, process an interlibrary loan, and draft the following semester's noncredit workshop brochure. Communication with the main campus is largely via e-mail and voicemail. Printed support materials covering every aspect of distance learning are available and updated regularly, and main-campus staff routinely travel to centers to provide direct support, backup, training, and teaching.

Funding is decentralized. Faculty salaries are included in division personnel budgets. Licensing and per-student fees, materials acquisition, technology support, and library and related services are funded by the Learning Resources budget. Academic Computing handles networking and the digital end of technology support. During 1991–94, Title III funds assisted with 56Kb lines, local- and wide-area networks, computers, library software, video enhancements, and the development of faculty training materials.

Instructional Strategies

Figure 6-1 shows a model of the relationships of location- and time-dependence or independence. In terms of time/place independence, Genesee made a specific effort to move toward the lower right quadrant with its distance learning options. The availability of technology resources and public utility partnerships assisted in this decision: voicemail and e-mail networks were in place, with the assistance of Title III-funded 56Kb lines and WANs. Connectivity and bandwidth for two-way video synchronous interaction were not deemed affordable without grant assistance. One such grant has since

Figure 6-1: **Relationship of Media to Venues of Instruction**

	PLACE-DEPENDENT	PLACE-INDEPENDENT
TIME-DEPENDENT (synchronous)	Conventional classroom instruction Scheduled tutorial	Specially equipped location (away from main campus): Live video/audioconference Live two-way video/audio Home- or workplace-based: Live (online) e-mail Broadcast/cablecast video Broadcast audio (radio) Either/both: Live one-way video/two-way audio
TIME-INDEPENDENT (asynchronous)	Mediated Learning Lab Audio/video (tape, disc), print, computer, "multimedia" Simulation, virtual reality, simulated travel Drop-in tutorial Site-based network/Internet/modem courses	Voicemail Home- or workplace-based: Data Network/BBS (VAX Notes; e-mail conference via LAN/WAN; modem courses; Internet courses Correspondence courses Independent/directed study Recorded (time-shifted) video/audio CAI/tutorial on diskette

been approved for funding during 1996, and will be used to move Genesee into synchronous instruction.

The metaphor for selecting, implementing, and training faculty and students in the use of various technologies is that of the "toolbox." The college provides the tools and instructions for their use. Faculty use them to construct whatever object (learning activities and sequences, behavioral outcomes, attitudes/understandings, skill sets) they have specified in their blueprint (syllabus).

Development of instruction is a faculty responsibility. Once courses and faculty assignments have been agreed on, faculty meet with the Learning Resources associate dean; Academic Computing; and library, media, and other support staff to ascertain best strategies for the content, learners, conditions, and instructor's style. The faculty member is provided with "instruction manuals" for the tools in the toolbox, provided access to equipment and resources and encouraged to use the distance learning tools. Benchmarks and timelines are established by means of a planning calendar. Syllabus construction is carefully monitored; support materials are assembled, edited, and cross-checked by the Learning Resources dean and secretary. Every attempt is made to provide copies of all course materials to all campus centers, via an indexed three-ring binder, at least two weeks prior to the start of every semester.

Current issues facing distance learning at Genesee include: What is a fair section size? The extra costs of licensing, per-student fees, technology, and staff support encourage economies of scale in distance learning offerings. With mean section sizes in the 27 to 29 range (40 to 45 percent above the institutional mean), distance learning courses are still not quite competitive with conventional courses on a cost-per-FTE basis.

Over 90 percent of Genesee distance learning students judge distance learning courses as "at least as rigorous" as conventional courses. This is not accomplished without significant and personal faculty involvement.

Keeping the program student-centered and vital as it "matures" has been an unexpected issue. Some faculty have taught the same distance learning course a dozen or more times. Support staff have identified and solved problems, written procedures, and codified policies which do not always work on students' behalf. Distance learning can become so well institutionalized that it loses its innovative cachet and some of the edge that made it attractive to students.

Technologies Employed

Video materials are purchased or satellite-downlinked, and duplicated (under license terms) in-house. For each course using videos, the main campus library and each campus center is issued one set of videos per course for on-site use, and one or more sets for student check-out, depending on local need. Except for in-house productions and some publisher-supplied videos, only students registered in licensed telecourses may use tapes. When a strong hardship case is made, students are issued their own set of tapes ($25 deposit held). Genesee is equipped to produce inexpensive medium-volume dubbing, and does not currently use a student tape-leasing service.

Genesee also feeds an educational access cable channel, and currently runs 15 to 18 hours per week of programming originating from campus. The cable service footprint roughly overlaps the college's service area; nearly 60 percent of students have potential cable access. Cablecast time of day is increasingly irrelevant, as most students use home VCRs to time-shift.

Audiocassettes, either locally produced or publisher-supplied and cleared for duplication, are part of some courses, notably Medical Terminology, and are available for check-out at all locations. Computer software supports many courses (such as Minitab for Statistics) and is similarly available.

A wide-area computer network allows distant students asynchronous access to instructors through computer labs at all campus locations as well as through limited dial-in. Students are issued VAX accounts and are trained in the use of e-mail and VAX Notes conferencing software in orientations held at each off-campus center weekday evenings and Saturdays, during the week before each semester begins.

Student Services Provided

Genesee strives to provide comparable student services to
all its students, regardless of location or instructional
delivery mode. A standard, color-coded syllabus
supplement is provided every semester to each student that
details current information common to all distance
learning courses. Supplemental information includes
contact names and phone numbers, hours of all support
locations, the academic calendar, and standard college
policies and procedures.

Textbooks, workbooks, and publisher-supplied print
materials are sold through the college bookstore and also can
be ordered at campus centers. Some instructors have
developed their own "CoursePaks" which are duplicated
locally and made available through the bookstore. (Faculty
may not profit from the sale of any course material.)

Syllabi and all other print materials are duplicated in the
college print shop. Some courses employ Hypertext diskettes
which contain a variety of information. All locally produced
materials are mailed to registered students 7 to 10 days
before the start of each semester. Biweekly updates catch
any late registrants.

A required first- or second-week review is held on the
main campus on the first or second Saturday of every
semester. Computer lab orientations are also held at this time,
with print material, tutorial handouts, and on-site staff
support widely available.

Advisors at all locations are routinely trained and updated
as to offerings, requirements, policies, and procedures.
Current print materials, course syllabi, and other support
materials are also provided at all locations. Questions by staff
and students are frequent and are addressed immediately via
phone, e-mail, and voicemail. A self-advising pamphlet is
widely disseminated.

All advisors (faculty, technical specialists/assistants, and
deans) have access to student records online, using Degree
Audit software. Instant information about academic records
and current status is available to advisors, as is information on
the progress-to-degree impact of any given course option.
Students also have personal access to their own information.

Support staff at all locations are aware of and trained to
deal with the special needs of distant students.
Records/Admissions, Financial Aid, Library,
Tutorial/Developmental Education, and other staff have all
developed appropriate materials and/or procedures for
distance learners.

A mandatory student orientation/review is held the first or
second Saturday morning of each semester, on the Batavia
main campus. Student information packets (described
previously) are mailed to registered students seven to 10 days
before the beginning of every semester. At the instructor's
discretion, receipt of this mailing marks the nominal start of
each course. The mandatory main-campus gathering is
therefore not an orientation but an opportunity for students
and instructors to meet face-to-face, review any questions
raised by close examination of the syllabus and course
materials, and for the first assignment(s) to be turned in.
Computer labs (e-mail and computer conferencing) and library

orientations are also scheduled during this three-hour period,
with faculty directing students where they need to go. The
bookstore and Records and Business offices are also open, as
is Student Activities, where photo-ID cards can be obtained
and used for accessing library and computer lab services.

On-time completion rates for students who attend these
sessions is higher than for those who do not, except in the case
of multiple course enrollees, who are familiar with procedures
and make other arrangements with faculty. Additional optional
orientations assist those students wishing to access computer
lab, library, tutoring, and testing services locally. Attendance
at these sessions correlates highly with student success.

Tutorial assistance is free at the main campus and all
centers, depending on available staff. All tutors are part-time
employees. Student access to staff is greatly enabled through a
general open-door policy and the informal style of nearly all
Genesee employees. Student e-mail and voicemail accounts
have also greatly democratized access to faculty and
management, and flattened any vertical organizational
structure. This enables close monitoring of student issues,
smoothing of procedural snags, and quality control.

Grading and Evaluation

Faculty set academic standards for distance learning offerings.
In all cases, they are encouraged to set them the same or
higher than for conventional courses. Objectives, evaluations,
projects, writing, labs, research, and all other aspects of
distance learning courses should be comparable in rigor to
those of conventional classes, and Genesee's success in this is
documented by 90 percent of responding students.

One of the many interesting paradigm shifts that has
occurred is how distance learning faculty look at student
participation. A Developmental Psychology course provides
an example. Meaningful, personally revealing discussion
occurs in a conventional classroom about the painful
experiences of adolescence from both a child's and a parent's
viewpoint. That discussion is of equal intensity and
instructional value when it occurs in a computer conference,
but it is different in important ways. Genesee faculty and
students have learned to value both.

Program outcomes are assessed formally by means of
tracking on-time completion rates, grading patterns, and
student survey instruments. Informal assessment is ongoing,
with adjustments as needed. Qualitative and demographic
information is systematically gathered and reported as part of
the 1991–94 Title III project requirements; since then,
assessment tools have been altered somewhat, in a direction
away from ensuring compliance and toward identifying needs
and growth areas.

Unique or Exemplary Practices

It may be useful to sum up what does *not* characterize
Genesee. One finds no single defining attribute, no one
high-tech solution, and no overarching, inflexible
pedagogical assumptions.

Genesee's uniqueness is in the diversity of tools, strategies,
and approaches used to provide and support distance learning

in a rural environment. It has enjoyed the luxury of building in quality support services, advising, faculty development, course design, and retention efforts, resulting in higher-than-normal on-time completion rates and faculty and student satisfaction indicators. The guiding philosophy has been that if quality is built in, the numbers will follow, and they have.

Genesee's distance learning efforts to this point have focused on asynchronous and place-independent delivery of credit courses to working adults. The college's broad menu of courses across the curriculum emphasize flexibility, a well-supported array of delivery options (tools in the toolbox), insistence on quality, faculty and departmental ownership of courses, academic rigor, attention to detail, and follow-through with both technology and student support services. As it matures and grows, Genesee's distance learning program will continue to be guided by student and curricular needs—and by practicality.

Robert G. Knipe
Associate Dean, Learning Resources
Genesee Community College
One College Road
Batavia, NY 14020
(716) 343-0055, x6595; fax: (716) 343-0433
e-mail: bobk@sgccvb.sunygenesee.cc.ny.us

Chapter 7

KIRKWOOD COMMUNITY COLLEGE
Cedar Rapids, Iowa

Norm Nielsen and Ellen J. Habel

Kirkwood Community College was established in 1966 in Cedar Rapids, Iowa, following enabling legislation for a statewide community college system in 1965. The legislation formed 15 community college districts that were to provide comprehensive educational services, including the first two years of college transfer work, postsecondary vocational-technical training, job training and retraining, high school completion programs, and continuing education opportunities.

Today, Kirkwood is the fifth largest institution of higher education in Iowa, with learning centers in each of its rural counties and Iowa City, and an enrollment of 10,026 students (fall 1995). The college serves a seven-county area with a total population of nearly 350,000.

Kirkwood offers more than 100 applied science, technology, and college-credit programs in addition to an extensive community and continuing education curriculum. Adult basic education and high school completion courses are provided to nearly 5,000 residents each year.

The Kirkwood Telecommunications System (KTS) was conceived in 1978 and funded from the college's capital construction funds and with the support of the Department of Commerce National Telecommunication and Information Administration Public Telecommunications Facilities program. The first of three stages of construction began in 1980.

Kirkwood's comprehensive, live, interactive distance learning network has grown from one class delivered to one location for 30 students to the multicomponent system it is today. From the establishment of the microwave transmission system and the Instructional Television Fixed Service (ITFS) system in 1981 to self-paced telecourses in the mid-1980s, to the satellite uplink in 1990, and the Iowa Communications Network in 1993, the college has maintained its commitment to overcoming barriers to education in East Central Iowa.

Kirkwood was one of the first educational institutions in the country to employ duplex microwave and ITFS to distribute live, two-way audio and video college-credit, continuing education, and high school courses to learning centers, high schools, and businesses. Currently, through these technologies—and the statewide fiber-optics network, the Iowa Communications Network—the college delivers an average of 55 college-credit courses and generates approximately 2,250 student registrations each semester.

Program Overview

Students Served and Programs Offered

KTS provides live, interactive instructional television courses over four networks. KTS courses serve primarily off-campus learning center students, who comprise 73 percent of total distance learning registrations. The average class size in the fall semester of 1995 was 41 students, and KTS registrations totaled 2,249 in 55 courses, an increase of two percent over 1994. Registrations have increased over 44 percent since 1992.

Students can earn A.A. degrees and degrees in 10 career option/business majors through instructional television. The college devotes two evenings per week to relicensure and recertification programs for professionals in health, banking, cosmetology, real estate, and insurance. Kirkwood is a full partner in providing shared high school programming and college-credit classes for high school students throughout the district.

Kirkwood also offers high school advanced placement courses, teacher in-service training, special event programming, and student service programs such as high school career exploration and adult student orientation. In addition, KTS is used for public service programming, such as the forums between farmers, financial institutions, and agricultural experts that took place during the farm crisis of the 1980s and the devastating flood of 1993.

Self-paced telecourses and a 21-community cable network deliver telecourses that generate an additional 1,300 student registrations each semester. Furthermore, the college regularly produces satellite conferences sponsored by the college and its public and private partners.

KTS serves a number of special populations as well, delivering credit courses to the Iowa State Men's Reformatory with return voice transmission, allowing reformatory students to interact with instructors and other students during class. Inmates at the Women's Correctional Facility and the Iowa Medical Classification Center also access the system.

Program Organization

Operation of the Kirkwood Telecommunications System requires the talents and cooperation of several departments within the college, particularly the Telecommunications Services Department, the Video and Media Services Department (part of the Computer Information Systems Division), and the Distance Learning Department (housed within the instructional branch of the college).

The Telecommunications Services Department is responsible for the development and implementation of new telecommunications projects and services including engineering design, equipment specifications, bidding processes, as well as installation, maintenance and repair of distance learning transmission technologies, FM radio station equipment, professional television production equipment, satellite uplink equipment, telephone PBX equipment, and audio-visual equipment. This department also ensures that all of the telecommunications systems under the jurisdiction of the Federal Communications Commission are in compliance with regulations. Furthermore, the director of telecommunications services represents the tele-communications interests of the college with staff, area businesses and industries, other telecommunications services, and the community.

The Video and Media Services Department includes the manager of media services; the KTS program manager, who acts as a liaison between technical engineering and instruction; and four part-time master control operators, who report to the program manager and execute the day-to-day functions of the system.

The Master Control Center is located on the main campus and controls all technical functions and support for each remote site. Here, 225 hours of programming each week are scheduled, executed, and logged for Federal Communications Commission compliance.

Instructional planning, class scheduling, and faculty and student support are provided by the staff of the Distance Learning Department. The director of distance learning is responsible for the administration, selection, scheduling, and marketing of KTS courses. Course schedules are planned two years in advance in cooperation with the college's associate deans and county directors.

The Distance Learning Department also selects interested faculty, both full- and part-time, to teach on KTS and provides them with orientation sessions essential for instruction on interactive television. Faculty are paid additional credits for teaching on KTS using the adjunct faculty salary schedule. The number of additional credits paid are based on the number of students enrolled in the class.

Two full-time office associates provide faculty support for instructors of KTS credit classes. The staff also supports each receive site with weekly materials such as exams, assignments, and system schedules. KTS is also used for regular meetings with site facilitators, maintaining an open avenue of communication to review, solve, and check any informational and delivery concerns.

Instructional Strategies

Instructors on the telecommunications system use course syllabi developed by the faculty from the academic departments as guides for the development of KTS courses. Textbooks and other instructional materials recommended by the academic departments are also used. In many cases, full-time faculty teach on-campus courses via KTS.

Each semester, the director of distance learning works with the KTS program manager to assist faculty in becoming familiar with the technology and specific techniques for teaching over the telecommunications system. Instructors participate in a four-hour program that includes topics such as course development, instructional strategies, off-campus centers, technology in the classroom, secretarial support, and expectations of students, staff, and faculty. Faculty are encouraged to solicit feedback from students early in the semester, and students are given the opportunity to share their perceptions of the course at the end of the term.

Technologies Employed

The college's primary delivery system is Telelink, a 12-gigahertz microwave network linking seven classrooms in outlying Kirkwood centers to the main campus in Cedar Rapids. Each microwave path carries video and audio signals in both directions simultaneously. Faculty can originate classes from any of the seven remote sites or from the main campus.

Telelink is used almost exclusively for college-credit classes. Over 70 hours of credit classes are offered each week, serving over 1,000 students in seven counties. Courses range from algebra and speech to criminology and human anatomy. Additional system space can accommodate up to 24 audio or data signals. Currently, the extra space carries voice and data to and from the remote sites.

At the same time the microwave transmission facilities were constructed, four ITFS transmitters were built on the Cedar Rapids campus, and six ITFS repeaters were located on the college's microwave tower sites within the six counties surrounding Cedar Rapids. Of the six outlying repeaters, four are configured to be ITFS transmitters as well as repeating the signal from a campus transmitter. This configuration allows the school district located at the repeater/transmitter site to tailor localized programming to their needs.

The 2.5-gigahertz broadcast television signal of the ITFS can be picked up from any line of sight within approximately 20 miles of the transmitter. Special FM radio response transmitters at the receive sites allow students to interact with the instructor via audio response.

The ITFS A-1 and A-2 channels (the Secondary School Network and the Urban Network) are programmed with live classes from 7 a.m. until 10 p.m., Monday through Friday, and from 8 a.m. until noon on Saturday. Of the two channels, A-1 is normally repeated throughout the seven-county area to 37 classrooms.

Currently, 29 elementary and secondary schools have equipped classrooms with ITFS reception and audio-response hardware. Through this network, schools receive college-credit courses and high school classes such as Russian cultures, environmental science, and technical mathematics. Because of expenses, limited enrollments, or other factors, these classes would not be offered at individual schools. Area principals and counselors jointly plan instructional offerings for which districts can cooperatively share instructional costs.

The Business and Industry Training Network is ITFS channel A-3. KTS receive sites have been installed at selected business locations in the Cedar Rapids area and the college's New Business Center, allowing employees at these sites to participate in both credit and noncredit offerings. This network is also used to deliver satellite videoconferences and serves as an important component of the Kirkwood satellite downlink service.

ITFS channel A-4, the college's cable television network, is programmed with telecourses and general interest programming. The Kirkwood channel can be seen in over

75,000 homes in 21 communities. Local cable companies access Kirkwood programming via the ITFS channel. The central objective of the cable television network is to offer college-credit telecourses in both semester and block formats. Block programming airs complete courses in one or two weeks, so students can record each program for later viewing. This allows students the convenience of earning college credit through home study at their own pace.

The cable channel also offers special and general interest programs, live college athletic events, and programs produced by students in the communications media program. Other features of the educational cable channel include public service programs of local interest and classic films. Programming from the Telelink and ITFS systems, as well as satellite events, can be fed through the cable network.

Kirkwood Community College has had an active role in the development of the Iowa Communications Network (ICN), the statewide fiber-optic network capable of transporting interactive audio, video, telephone, and data signals. The first fiber-optic cable for the network was buried in 1991 and the system now reaches at least one educational endpoint in each of the state's 99 counties. The entire network is interconnected so any site can originate and feed to any or all of the endpoints. The backbone of the ICN connects the state's 15 community colleges, Iowa Public Television, the Iowa National Guard Armory in Des Moines, and the three state universities. Each community college serves as a regional hub, and when the network is complete, it will include high schools, area education agencies, and selected public libraries, hospitals, and private colleges.

Kirkwood uses the ICN as an additional delivery system for video-based live, interactive credit or noncredit classes, as well as other educational telecommunications traffic. Classes originating outside the Kirkwood service area, including upper division and graduate coursework from the state's public universities, can also be routed to Kirkwood facilities via this network. Likewise, any Kirkwood class can be transmitted to any other ICN site in the state.

Satellite videoconferencing benefits many on-campus departments and organizations, in addition to local and regional businesses and groups. Using satellite receive dishes and an on-campus distribution network, programs can be sent to meeting rooms of various sizes. Programs received via satellite allow students to gain college and continuing education credits or to interact in national events. Satellite programs can also be sent out over the microwave, ITFS, and ICN systems on either a live or delayed basis.

Kirkwood's satellite uplink facilities are available for delivery of selected college activities or as a community service. Through this uplink, programming can be delivered on a national or international basis. The college also serves as an anchor site for the Community College Satellite Network (CCSN). Through CCSN, selected programs and services of interest are offered to other community colleges.

All KTS classrooms are designed to meet the specific needs of a televised class. The four origination classrooms on the main campus accommodate 25 students each. The off-campus Telelink sites use standard size classrooms similarly equipped for program origination.

Origination classrooms are equipped with a moveable camera in the back of the room focused on the instructor and a front camera fixed on the students. Students communicate with the instructor using a table-top switch-activated microphone. KTS staff perform all technical operations for the entire course; assist in the set-up of visual aids; operate video, audio, and switching equipment; and act as a buffer between the instructor and technology.

The main campus classrooms are automated, allowing the instructor to operate front, rear, and overhead cameras from one convenient console. Instructors can switch between remote sites and classroom cameras and operate the overhead camera to accommodate various support visuals. Other media such as computers, videodiscs, videotape, films, slides, transparencies, charts, and models are also incorporated in the KTS classrooms.

Student Services Provided

Kirkwood's county learning centers are at the heart of support services for distance learners. A total of 75 self-paced, face-to-face, and KTS courses are offered at each county center each semester. Students can earn all of the necessary credits for an associate's degree by taking classes within 30 miles of their homes.

At each center, a county director provides professional, personalized support and services such as academic advising, tutoring, testing, career and job skills counseling, and financial aid. Students can register for credit, community education, and high school completion courses at their local center. The centers also offer an online library search and request service, computers for student use, and can receive tuition for any college class. Weekly meetings with the Distance Learning Department and KTS staff provide an open forum for communication, planning, and idea sharing among county directors and the main campus of the college.

Student Grading and Program Evaluation

Student progress in KTS classes is measured and grades are assigned in the same manner as traditional courses. Assignments, tests, and quizzes are sent to instructors and returned to students via first-class mail or facsimile machines.

Outcome measurements include classroom observations, surveys of student perceptions of teaching, and grade distribution reports. On-going communication among the director of distance learning, county directors, and associate deans ensures the highest quality of instruction.

Unique or Exemplary Practices

Kirkwood used the Iowa Communications Network to develop the nation's first statewide articulated program in Fire Science. In April 1993, the college expanded its Fire Science certificate program to an A.S./career option degree. Students throughout Iowa can earn the degree by combining general education and business management classes at their local community college with Kirkwood's technical courses. Kirkwood delivers two of the seven required technical courses over ICN each semester during evening hours and currently has agreements with eight four-year institutions in Iowa and Illinois to accept the Fire Science associate's degree into their bachelor programs. The Iowa State University Extension's Fire Science bookstore provides one-day order processing and shipment to any location in the state. A career mentoring program and electronic bulletin board service for student advising complete the program.

This program illustrates the value of distance learning in improving the accessibility and efficiency of education. From 1992 to 1995, the number of students enrolled in the program increased from 53 to over 250. These students would not have access to an associate's degree program in Fire Science without the ICN and the cooperation of the state's community colleges. Furthermore, the increase in demand has been met without adding staff members in the fire science program at Kirkwood or any of the other community colleges in Iowa. The college is currently exploring adaptation of the fire science model to international marketing.

Kirkwood continues to pursue new methods of reaching learners through technology. The college is a partner in both The International Community College, a project of the League for Innovation in the Community College, and The World Community College, which was initiated by Community Colleges for International Development. Both of these collaborative efforts will offer programs anywhere in the world, regardless of geographic or political boundaries. Both have also committed to maintaining flexibility through the use of established and emerging technologies.

Participation in endeavors such as these maintains Kirkwood's edge in providing accessible, quality education and training in response to community needs, as the college mission mandates. As technology advances, the community and the community's needs expand and diversify. Kirkwood stands ready to meet those local and global challenges.

Norm Nielsen, President
Kirkwood Community College
6301 Kirkwood Boulevard SW
Cedar Rapids, IA 52404
(319) 398-5500; fax: (319) 398-5502
e-mail: nnielsen@kirkwood.cc.ia.us

Ellen J. Habel, Grants Development Officer
Kirkwood Community College
6301 Kirkwood Boulevard SW
Cedar Rapids, IA 52404
(319) 398-5500; fax: (319) 398-5502
e-mail: ehabel@kirkwood.cc.ia.us

Chapter 8

MIAMI-DADE COMMUNITY COLLEGE DISTRICT
Miami, Florida

Judy Lever-Duffy

Miami-Dade Community College is a multicampus community college encompassing five campuses and district operations that together serve metropolitan Dade County in South Florida. The college offers approximately 145 A.A., A.S., and certificate programs to some 125,000 credit and noncredit students annually. The mission of the college is to provide accessible, affordable, high-quality education by keeping the learner's needs at the center of decision making and working in partnership with its dynamic, multicultural community. To that end, the college's goals, objectives, offerings, and operations reflect the strengths inherent in its internal and external diversity.

Miami-Dade is the largest single community college in the country. In the college's 34-year history, it has awarded approximately 144,500 degrees and certificates and has the distinction of conferring more degrees to minority students than any other college in the country. As an open-door institution, Miami-Dade accepts all students, whatever their entering level of basic skill. It assists each student to prepare for college-level courses as necessary and strives to empower every student at every level to achieve their personal academic goals.

The college is an integral part of the community it serves. Over 75 percent of Dade County public high school graduates planning to attend college in Florida elect to attend Miami-Dade. During any given year, one of every six families in Dade County has a family member enrolled at Miami-Dade in either credit or noncredit courses. In a recent poll, a strong majority of Dade County voters thought the college very important to the welfare of their families and their community. More telling than words are the actions of a community. On September 8, 1992, only two weeks after Hurricane Andrew devastated so many homes and disrupted so many lives in Dade County, voters went to the polls and approved by a two-to-one margin a referendum to provide the college with additional funding. Clearly, the people of Dade County understand that Miami-Dade is a true *community* college, and support it accordingly.

Program Overview

Distance education at Miami-Dade has a long and varied history. The college has repeatedly demonstrated its ability and desire to meet student needs through innovative approaches to alternative delivery. This is evidenced by the array of diverse distance and alternative learning programs in place across the campuses.

The college's distance and alternative delivery programs include Internet-based independent-study courses, Open

College courses featuring telecourses enhanced by multimedia technologies, Life Lab courses that emphasize interdisciplinary flexible delivery, Facilitated Learning courses with modular, technology-intensive support on-campus and off-campus, and Virtual Workshops featuring distance-delivered continuing education.

Courses offered through these programs include core curricula in English, humanities, math, science, and social science, as well as a broad range of business and technology courses. While most students elect to use alternative and distance-delivery courses for only part of their A.A. and A.S. degrees, it is possible to complete the entire degree through some of these programs.

Each campus has been free to develop and implement alternative programs appropriate to the needs of the students it serves and the talents of its faculty. From full-production telecourses such as *The Art of Being Human* to single campus course offerings, the college has provided flexible and appropriate access to those students who cannot or prefer not to participate in traditional on-campus courses. In the 1995–96 academic year, the college expects to serve over 1,000 students through these varied and rich alternatives.

Program Organization

Currently, each campus has the option to design and implement an organizational structure to administer distance and alternative delivery programs. While this has made the campus programs responsive and flexible, the impact of the changes and capabilities of emerging technologies has altered the environment in which they are implemented. These changes have caused college leadership to initiate a comprehensive and strategic review of distance and alternative delivery at the college.

During 1994–95, the college created an Ad-Hoc Technology Goals Committee which had, as a part of its charge, a preliminary review of distance education at the college. This committee recommended that a permanent collegewide Technology Committee be established with a distance education subcommittee created to advise the college on distance-delivery matters. In late 1995, the Technology Committee was established by action of the college's new administration led by district president, Eduardo J. Padrón. One of the Technology Committee's first actions was the establishment of the distance education subcommittee.

The distance education subcommittee is charged with the review of current practices in distance delivery, examination of organizational options, and aiding faculty in augmenting their curriculum via distance delivery within the framework of the existing and emerging technology options. Finally, the distance education subcommittee is charged with making appropriate recommendations to the Technology Committee as to the strategic direction for distance education at the college.

Instructional Strategies

Current campus distance and alternative delivery programs use both synchronous and asynchronous approaches to distance delivery. Across the campuses, the distance and alternative delivery program's synchronous instructional strategies include on-site meetings and seminars, audioconferencing, computer-based chat modes, and student testing. On-campus meetings and seminars require that students attend either the home campus offering the program or one of the other campuses with which the home campus is working collaboratively. Such seminars are used for direct instruction, small group interaction, content review, evaluations, or academic support. Faculty may schedule mandatory seminars at specific points during the semester or may offer them as optional opportunities depending on the structure of the course and the parameters of the campus program. In some programs, students can request peer study groups which may be implemented through the seminar format.

Audioconferencing includes both group telephone conferences and individual telephone meetings between teacher and student. Using this instructional strategy, some campuses use the telephone for group activities such as conferences, cooperative learning groups, group discussion, and direct instruction of small groups. Typical is the small group meeting to discuss an issue or topic that has previously been sent via mail, fax, or e-mail to several students. Faculty facilitate group interaction.

Real-time computer-based discussion is one of the newer instructional strategies on the campuses. Using conferencing software or Internet chat mode, students interact with each other and the instructor. This strategy is in its early stages of integration into curriculum and to date has been included in a limited number of distance and alternative delivery courses.

Asynchronous strategies are those that are time-shifted. At Miami-Dade, these include instruction via bulletin board systems, computer conferencing, and e-mail on the college network or the Internet; prerecorded video and/or audio lectures and presentations; interactive learning guides; and multimedia CD-ROM or disk-based instruction. All campuses have included print-based learning guides and prerecorded video and audio within their course strategies. Some campuses have prepared instructional materials and tutorials via multimedia authoring systems. Additionally, packaged, run-time instructional presentations have been created and provided to students to assist them in mastering course competencies. Campuses using this type of asynchronous strategy make these materials available to students in campus labs, on CD-ROMs, on disk, and in some cases, online.

For campuses that have extensively integrated computer technology into their distance and alternative delivery programs, online interaction and instruction has become a critical instructional strategy. Examples of activities supported through this type of strategy include collaborative writing, online discussion groups, research activities in groups or individually, and question and answer sessions.

Emphasis in many of these programs is on providing a highly interactive environment through the use of the many technologies available across the college. All programs employ student-centered approaches that reflect the common goal of meeting the needs of a diverse population of students through flexible instruction that overcomes the constraints of time and/or place boundaries. All campuses have encouraged the restructuring of curriculum to accommodate the instructional strategies available for these flexible program. One campus has developed and implemented a specific instructional design for courses offered through distance and alternative delivery.

Technologies Employed

The campuses use the full gambit of distance-delivery technologies in their varied distance and alternative delivery programs. All campuses use print and prerecorded video as a base technology tool to deliver instruction and maximize access. Print and videocassettes are available at all campuses through the Learning Resource Centers and through the Audio-Visual Departments. The college no longer uses video broadcast within any of its programs. Prohibitive cost and student preference for cassettes caused the college to discontinue emphasis on broadcast. Since the college serves a densely populated metropolitan area and since the strategic placement of the campuses make them easily accessible to all population centers, broadcast of video components in distance education programs was determined to be unnecessary.

Audio technologies are used extensively by campus programs. Prerecorded audiocassettes have provided commentary, panel discussions, and taped lecture for students in many of the programs. Phone conferences provide synchronous interaction while voicemail provides asynchronous opportunities to interact with instructors. Some campuses have created instructional voicemail accounts on which students can access course information or instructional components and leave questions, comments, or even respond to verbal assignments.

Computer technologies are used by a number of campuses. Electronic mail is used to provide interaction between faculty and students and among students in a course. E-mail has been used by one campus to create a "paperless" English Composition Course and by another to create listserv-type discussion groups. Electronic bulletin board systems and computer conferencing systems are used by some of the campuses to provide access to course information, to conduct asynchronous discussions, and to provide students not currently enrolled with an opportunity to visit and explore courses that might be of interest. Faxes, both through the network and via stand-alone fax machines, are used for interaction, feedback, and formative evaluation on some of the campuses. The Internet is used for electronic mail and as a resource for academic coursework. The Internet, available through the local freenet (SEFLIN), through the Florida Instructional Resource Network (FIRN), through a host of private providers and commercial services, or through the collegewide network, is used by distance and alternative delivery faculty to broaden access to distance resources. In the college's multicultural and international setting, the application of Internet-related resources to instruction has provided unique benefits.

The distance education subcommittee has appointed a telecommunications task force to review existing systems and make recommendations for the use of compressed video in distance and alternative delivery. The college has had an administrative compressed video network in place for some years. Currently, the task force is exploring both stand-alone compressed video systems and those that can be fully integrated into the existing collegewide network. Additionally, the task force is reviewing document sharing systems supported by an enhanced phone bridge for use in distance delivery. While these systems may or may not support video images of the participants, several campuses have concluded that they would prefer to use a system that provides synchronous sharing of documents and presentation materials.

All campuses use a variety of technologies in the implementation of distance and alternative delivery programs. While the availability of specific technologies varies by campus, each campus' distance and alternative delivery program effectively uses the technologies at hand. In each program, the technologies implemented provide alternatives for access, interaction, and learning in an effort to meet the diverse needs, technological competencies, and learning styles of the students.

Student Services Provided

Miami-Dade has a collegewide, telephone-based registration system in place that is used by all campus distance and alternative delivery programs. Students can access the college's online registration system at each campus and can interact with financial aid and student services advisors. Some of the campus distance and alternative delivery programs have enhanced these student services systems through the addition of support through voicemail, e-mail, and bulletin board systems. Information is "posted" on these systems and opportunities to respond or leave questions are provided. Both faculty and student services staff use these additional systems to interact with students and respond asynchronously to their needs.

Faculty and paraprofessionals offer additional academic support for the distance and alternative delivery programs. Some campuses schedule fixed office hours on-site while others use technology to offer support that is not place-bound. Telephone, computer chat modes, and phone conferencing are used to help students requiring assistance. On-campus learning and student support facilities are used by most campuses to provide support for distance and alternative delivery students when the instructor is not available, when additional tutoring is necessary, or when students need college information. Several campuses have created campuswide open technology labs or "computer courtyards" through which students can access online services and instruction at their convenience.

Electronic advisement, registration, and financial aid counseling are currently under development and will soon be available online. Site-based seminars are used by some of the programs to offer additional small group academic support. At least one campus is in the process of making such seminars computer-based.

Student Grading and Program Evaluation

Campus distance and alternative delivery programs reflect the same departmental standards that can be found among the other academic departments across the college. Each program is consistent with and in compliance with the grading and evaluation standards and procedures in place on the respective campus. For those campus programs that are run collaboratively with other academic departments, testing, grading, and evaluation in the distance and alternative delivery component are the same as would be found in the department itself.

Typically, students come to campus for testing. All campus programs offer testing at the home campus and some offer testing at campuses that are collaboratively offering a specific course or program. Student evaluation and grade assignment at all campuses is consistent with departmental, campus, and college standards.

Distance and alternative delivery programs at all campuses are evaluated through the standard collegewide course and instructor evaluation procedures developed by the Centers for Teaching and Learning. The instrument used is a collegewide standard for traditional courses and is applied to alternative programs as well. In addition to the collegewide evaluation, some campuses have created and implemented additional course and program evaluations. These summative evaluations are used to provide data on which program adjustments and course revisions can be made.

Unique or Exemplary Practices

Miami-Dade Community College is well known for its focus on excellence in teaching and learning. To that end, the college has provided a broad base of professional development opportunities in several areas associated with distance and alternative learning. In accordance with its emphasis on training, the college has provided faculty and staff opportunities to learn about and pilot potential distance-delivery technologies within their own courses and participate as both faculty and students in distance education experiences.

Each campus offers faculty extensive training opportunities in the use and application of delivery technologies. These workshops and subsequent development experiences with mentors have resulted in the creation of a variety of distance and alternative learning instructional tools. From multimedia course tutorial development to instructional design for computer-mediated courses to the use and application of the Internet, these training experiences have empowered faculty to embrace technology and apply it to both synchronous and asynchronous instruction. Without the training and support offered through this extensive professional development program, faculty could not have been so collectively prepared across the college to create the variety of courses included in the college's distance and alternative learning programs.

In 1995, Miami-Dade was awarded one of the four Florida State University System grants in distance learning. Ranked number one among the applicants, the college proposed the creation of a Virtual Workshop to teach faculty to use distance education via asynchronous distance delivery. The design and materials for the Virtual Workshop serve to teach as well as model distance-delivery techniques. The workshop, now completed and in pilot across all campuses, is one more example of the opportunity to learn about and experience distance delivery, and the first of many that will enable more faculty and staff to participate in the college's extensive professional development opportunities.

The college's commitment to appropriately prepare faculty and staff for technology and for the distance and alternative delivery strategies it supports has facilitated innovation. One such innovation has given training a new twist. Technology readiness has been taken a step further at one of the campuses; it has been expanded to include not only faculty and staff readiness but also student readiness. A student technology skills course has been developed and implemented. The course, offered asynchronously primarily on-campus, offers students an opportunity to obtain competency in the technology skills they need for participation in both traditional and alternative delivery courses. This course uses the instructional model developed for the campus' distance and alternative delivery program. The innovation of this campus is another example of the college's collective emphasis on adequate training and preparation of all participants in distance delivery.

Miami-Dade's commitment to the preparation of the college community is well known. The college's human support structure is dedicated to people and to empowering them with the training that is critical for the future. For distance education and alternative delivery programs, commitment to training and support has made it possible for the college to generate innovation at every campus. Through it, the college has moved beyond the traditional applications of leading-edge technology into the implementation of innovative instruction. This commitment evidences the value the college places on people and is one of its most exemplary practices. The college's respect for the diversity, capacity, and potential of its students, faculty, and staff is the key that will enable Miami-Dade to maintain its prominence among community colleges.

Judy Lever-Duffy, Chair
Collegewide Distance Education Committee
Director, Information Technology Center
Miami-Dade Community College District
Homestead Campus
500 College Terrace
Homestead, FL 33030
(305) 237-5074; fax: (305) 237-5002
e-mail: lever-h@mdcc.edu

Chapter 9

Northern Virginia Community College
Annandale, Virginia

Randal A. Lemke

Northern Virginia Community College (NVCC), in the suburbs of Washington, D.C., consists of five full-service campuses and the Extended Learning Institute (ELI), which is the college's unit for distance education. It is one of the 23 colleges of the Virginia Community College System (VCCS) and since its founding in 1964, NVCC has grown to be the largest institution of higher education in Virginia. In the fall of 1995, it had over 38,000 students with 2,200 students of these involved in distance education.

The Extended Learning Institute was formed in 1975 to serve students who could not, or preferred not to, attend classes on campus. From its origins, it was designed as a home-study program based on asynchronous learning. It also began as a continuous enrollment program where students could begin their studies at any point in the semester. These two elements remain at the center of ELI today as it provides students opportunities to participate in higher education while maintaining professional and personal commitments. This provision of access is congruent with the college's open admissions policy and is responsive to students who live in the fast-paced and traffic-choked environs of Washington, D.C.

Throughout its existence, ELI adopted new instructional technologies as they became available as common consumer products. It began with print-based materials and added broadcast TV, cable TV, audiocassettes, videotapes, personal computers, and voicemail as these technologies entered mainstream use.

In its early years, ELI designed courses in a systems development model that used content experts and instructional technologists who collaborated to provide teaching faculty with the course materials for delivery. That model has evolved along with the technology it employed and currently, recruitment and retention of faculty have been much more successful since they are now highly involved in the development of courses as well as in the teaching. Approximately 80 courses are taught at ELI each semester and summer by over 40 faculty members. Presently, there is a growing list of faculty who want to teach in distance education but who must wait until ELI can devote staff time to develop the courses.

Recently, ELI developed two degree programs and is working on a third. A.S. degree programs in Business Administration and General Studies were developed with the assistance of the Annenberg/CPB project in its New Pathways to a Degree Program. At present, a transfer-oriented engineering degree is being developed through funding of the Alfred P. Sloan Foundation in a program of grant projects to develop asynchronous learning networks. ELI is also a "Going the Distance" college, an effort by the PBS Adult Learning Services to develop degree programs in distance education. Within the VCCS, it has been designated as a Center for Distance Education and will assist its neighboring community colleges to provide distance education courses.

Program Overview

Students Served and Programs Offered

ELI's students live in one of the most vibrant economic areas in the United States and find themselves in a fast-paced life of work and family. The Virginia suburbs grew rapidly in the last 30 years, especially in the 1980s. Companies located in the new "fringe cities" of Tysons Corner, Rosslyn, Reston, Ballston, and other locations have transformed Northern Virginia from a bedroom community to a leading center of employment.

Most area residents work in the service economy. The area has a high number of college graduates, and most new jobs are in the information and communications sectors which demand a highly literate work force. ELI serves students in this environment through distance education even though most students live within 10 to 15 miles of one of NVCC's campuses. Geographic separation is not the issue for these students; rather, it is the need to be able to fit a college education into their busy professional and personal lives.

ELI students take courses for degree completion, personal enrichment, and to improve professional skills. In any one semester, about half of all ELI students take courses only via distance learning. Of these students, about six percent are new to the college. ELI both brings new students to the college and provides students an opportunity to mix on-campus and distance education courses to move more quickly through their courses of study.

ELI students, like most distance education participants nationally, are a few years older than their campus counterparts. At ELI, 37 percent of all students are 25 to 34 years of age. In that age bracket, students taking only ELI courses outnumber those taking a mix of ELI and campus courses. This group of people is starting careers and families, and ELI is an important opportunity for them to participate in higher education. Women, for whom these professional and personal commitments seem to be especially complex, participate in ELI more often than their male counterparts (66 to 34 percent while the college as a whole is 54 percent female).

ELI offers a primarily transfer-oriented program with 80 courses in accounting, art, biology, business, chemistry, computer information systems, economics, engineering, English, foreign languages, marketing, mathematics, office technology, philosophy, physics, psychology, sociology, speech, and student development. Along with an independent-study course in physical education from the Annandale campus, students can take all of their degree requirements for an A.S. in General Studies or Business Administration through ELI, as well as a certificate in Professional Writing for Business, Government and Industry.

Most courses do not require any campus visits other than to take examinations at one of the five campus testing centers. Science courses with laboratory and a speech course have from one to four required campus class sessions. Most labs can be completed at home or out in the community, but the few which require equipment or need to be supervised for safety reasons are done on campus. Speech classes convene to make presentations to a group of peers. The limited number of campus visits is not seen as a great problem because almost all students live in the Washington area—ELI does not market outside of Northern Virginia.

While the majority of ELI's programs are directed to Northern Virginia citizens, a new venue is developing. Through cooperative arrangements with other VCCS colleges, ELI is delivering and receiving asynchronous and synchronous courses through the Virginia Distance Education Network (VDEN). Participating colleges offer courses to other VCCS colleges. A mechanism has been established for delivering instruction and splitting revenue. ELI was selected as one of five VCCS Centers for Distance Education (CDE) and is charged to provide its neighboring community colleges assistance in delivering distance education. Currently, a two-way compressed video network is deployed at the five CDE colleges and in the summer of 1996, the compressed video network was expanded to all 23 VCCS colleges and 38 campuses and centers. NVCC and its sister VCCS schools are also in a cooperative agreement with Old Dominion University (ODU) through its Teletechnet program, allowing ODU to use some community college campus facilities to present its upper-division degree programs via a satellite downlink and telephonic return communication. Many of the Old Dominion students take lower-division courses at the VCCS colleges, then complete a bachelor's degree through ODU on the same campus.

Program Organization

ELI is an administrative unit that works cooperatively with the five NVCC campuses. All academic authority for ELI's courses resides within the campus divisions. ELI does not have faculty assigned to it; rather, instructors are chosen from the campuses to teach part of their load at ELI. Usually three to four adjunct lecturers teach with ELI, but to do so they are hired by the campus divisions and assigned to ELI. Faculty come from all five campuses, and credit for student enrollments is returned to their home campuses.

A faculty member is typically joined by an instructional technologist, a video producer, computer technicians, and clerical staff to constitute a course development team. The instructional technologist is either an academically trained instructional designer or a master teacher who has developed design skills from experience. The video producer has academic training in television production and experience adapting this knowledge to instructional video. Computer

technicians are assigned to install hardware and software systems, to maintain the computer conferencing systems, and to assist faculty in using the technology. Finally, the clerical staff prepares and copy edits manuscripts and makes arrangements for duplication of course materials.

In this mode, the faculty member is the sole determinant of what is taught and what the standards are for student success. The instructional technologist is a consultant to the faculty on distance education techniques. Similarly, the computer technicians and video producers provide advice and training to the faculty so they can use the technologies efficiently without having to learn to do so by trial and error.

Delivery of these courses brings together a different group of people to support the faculty member. Typically clerical personnel, the computer technician, testing center personnel, and occasionally the instructional technologist work with the faculty member to run the course. Testing center personnel administer and send exams to ELI for professors to grade. Clerical personnel sort faculty mail, file student exams, maintain student records on the college student information system, and staff a hotline where students can call for assistance on administrative issues. The computer technician maintains the computer conferencing server and troubleshoots modem and communication problems for students. In a limited number of courses, a student tutor is hired to assist the faculty member and students. The instructional technologist is called on if an unforeseen difficulty arises and the faculty member needs help devising a strategy to resolve the problem.

Through these support systems, faculty members are freed from administrative trivia and given professional and technical support to develop and deliver courses. ELI has six instructional technologists, a video producer, two computer technicians, and seven clerical support personnel on staff. In addition, the program can draw on the services of the college's Telecommunications Center and the campus testing centers.

Faculty teaching at ELI apply teaching credits towards their regular teaching load or for overload. No matter how many courses a faculty member teaches, all enrollment for each faculty member is collapsed together to determine how many courses it equates to. The scale is:

- 25 – 59   students equals 1.0 course
- 60 – 90   students equals 2.0 courses
- 91 – 105   students equals 2.5 courses
- 106 – 120   students equals 3.0 courses
- 121 – 135   students equals 3.5 courses
- 136 – 150   students equals 4.0 courses

The student FTEs are credited to the faculty member's campus division to support the staffing contribution. Operating funds to support these students are credited to ELI and constitute its annual budget.

Instructional Strategies

Distance education at NVCC is described as home study because the intent of college founders and president was to make every home in Northern Virginia a classroom. In 1975, this was ambitious thinking, but it did have precedent at the British Open University and the extension colleges of U.S. land grant universities.

This goal was furthered by a continuous enrollment format to give NVCC students expanded access to higher education. Students can enroll and begin working on courses any day of the year and have 16 weeks to complete their work. ELI will usually enroll 15 to 20 percent of its students after the drop and add process has been completed for campus sections. Procedures for this enrollment have been developed with campus registrars, and programming was written to accommodate it on the college student information system. With continuous enrollment, faculty find themselves working with students who are in different places in the course; on any one day faculty may grade papers from the first assignment, or a final exam. ELI maintains its own microcomputer-based student information system to help faculty keep track of students' progress and to send periodic progress reminders to students.

The fixed class dates and times of synchronous instruction are not compatible with continuous enrollment; almost all ELI courses are asynchronous. Students communicate with faculty and each other on an as-needed basis when it is convenient to them. Voicemail and computer conferencing are primarily the technologies students use to interact with faculty members because they can use them any time of the day or night.

During the last three years, ELI redeveloped all of its courses to make them eligible for inclusion in federal financial-aid calculations. To do so, ELI added telecommunication technologies to all courses. As faculty began using more video, audio, and computer technologies, the amount of communication between faculty and students increased. In so doing, ELI moved farther away from being an independent-study program. Faculty are proactive in communicating with students, sending welcome letters to get them started and reminders to keep them working. While the role of print materials is still vital, faculty now use more frequent and direct contact with students.

Technologies Employed

ELI chooses information technologies that are available in students' homes. Just as it adopted cable TV when it became widespread, ELI will incorporate multimedia when sufficient numbers of students have computers with CD-ROMs and sound systems. Currently, ELI does not employ multimedia (two or more media controlled by a microcomputer); rather it uses multiple media (two or three technologies that are not run by the same hardware) within a course. These technologies usually transmit course content or are the means of interactivity. When faculty members begin to develop courses they are asked to match the needs of their disciplines with the various technologies available. If they choose computer technology, they can use it for computer conferencing, for computer-assisted instruction, or for computer practice sets. If they choose audio technologies, they can record audiotapes to provide students with the content of the course, an outline of the course procedures, an advanced organizer to help them conceptualize the content, or they may use the tapes for a combination of these purposes. Faculty choose voicemail for conferencing, (where students hear and leave recorded messages on a course topic, similar to computer conferencing), or as a recorder of oral assignments, which is especially valuable in foreign language courses and speech.

Video courses use licensed telecourses from PBS and other vendors, NVCC's own productions of telecourses, video provided by textbook publishers, or a combination of two or more of these options. In the new CDE synchronous courses shared with VCCS colleges, a VTEL compressed video system is used over ISDN lines to support point-to-point and multipoint two-way interactive television. Whatever technology faculty choose, ELI's instructional technologists provide training and assistance.

With all the tools available to faculty, no two ELI courses look the same; faculty make different choices according to the needs of their discipline and their personal ease in using the technologies. All courses follow a standard 14- to 16-page "boilerplate" for the syllabus that students receive upon registration and a course guide (20–100 pages) that students buy along with required textbooks.

Student Services Provided

For the most part, ELI relies on the campuses for the provision of student services. Since most students live close by, they can take occasional advantage of the services provided on campus. All career and academic counseling is done by faculty and staff at the student's home campus where students also buy books and use the learning resource center, testing center, tutoring, and other campus student development services. When ELI began to offer degree programs, it worked more closely with each campus and developed new means to make sure that students were knowledgeable about the services of the college and could take advantage of them.

Admission to the college and registration for ELI classes can be done through the campuses or directly with ELI. Students can enroll via telephone or can mail or hand-deliver registrations to ELI. A course syllabus and directions on how to get started are mailed or given to the student at the time of registration. Students new to ELI either attend an on-campus orientation meeting or view and respond to an orientation program shown on cable TV.

ELI students are given a hotline number they can call to talk to an instructor concerning academic issues or reach staff members for other matters. Students can also get information from ELI's voicemail system which contains recorded messages on the most common topics of concern to students. Faculty members are required to be at ELI for specified office hours. Meetings on campus or at ELI can be arranged, and students are always encouraged to contact an instructor for help.

Student Grading and Program Evaluation

To evaluate students' work, faculty are encouraged to include several assignments and three to four exams in each course. They are also encouraged to make the exams count for most of the course grade or to require that students pass a majority of the exams in order to pass the course. The reliance on exams stems from the fact that these proctored sessions are the only times that the college is absolutely sure who is doing the assigned work. Finally, faculty are urged to use constructed response questions on exams and are discouraged from using only multiple-choice items. At the request of an instructor or an instructional technologist, ELI will conduct an item analysis of multiple-choice exam questions to identify bad questions.

When a student has completed all course requirements, the faculty member gives the grade to ELI's support personnel who post it on the college student information system. Grade reports are sent out periodically, and a transcript can be processed immediately.

Individual course evaluation is done via a student end-of-course survey on what they liked and disliked about the course. Additionally, analyses of grade distributions are used to see how ELI courses compare to campus courses and to determine where students were having the most difficulty. Occasionally, when a high withdrawal rate is noted, ELI staff conduct a quick telephone survey to determine if it was a problem with the course or if students had other circumstances that caused them to withdraw. Occasionally, ELI schedules student focus group discussions which provide a great amount of useful information.

Unique or Exemplary Practices

The Extended Learning Institute and the engineering, science, and mathematics faculty of NVCC's Annandale Campus are participating in the second phase of a project funded by the Sloan Foundation for the development of an engineering degree program offered through asynchronous learning networks (ALN). These computer networks are designed to reduce the isolation of home-study students by giving them a means to communicate with peers and faculty members while providing them the freedom to schedule their studies around their professional and personal lives.

Computer networks can reach into homes or businesses and, when used in asynchronous modes, provide students access to courses that are neither time- nor place-bound. When employed with instructional strategies that promote collaboration among classmates, these asynchronous networks offer the promise of a robust learning environment while maintaining the flexibility of home study.

In the first phase of this project, ELI developed four courses: two engineering, one calculus, and one chemistry course. It created an instructional model that used off-the-shelf technology to provide these asynchronous learning opportunities for NVCC students. A major result of Phase I was the demonstration that higher-order mathematics, science, and engineering courses could be taught in a home-study mode. Suitable administrative and instructional arrangements were made so that students visited campus as few as three to four times for taking examinations in the engineering and calculus courses, and eight to twelve times to take exams and perform labs in the chemistry course. Student enrollment in the first four home-study courses of this project exceeded ELI's expectations, with over 100 students registered in the four courses.

The most profound conclusion drawn from Phase I is that in order to obtain the level of communication inherently possible in an ALN, it is necessary to move farther away from the traditional ELI instructional model. Instruction in the past has been based on home study, continuous enrollment, independent learning, and a technology configuration designed to match that which is available to community college students. Phase II continues to be based on home study and a suitable technology platform, but it replaces independent learning with collaborative learning and it replaces continuous enrollment with regular registration where all students begin and end on the same date.

Phase II of this project is centered on five activities: 1) revision of the instructional model to produce a more robust ALN by requiring all students to use it and by grouping students to facilitate its use; 2) development of 10 additional courses in mathematics, physics, chemistry, and engineering to complete the full-degree offerings; 3) refinement of the computer conferencing system, based on FirstClass™ to maximize participation in the ALN activities while maintaining a similar amount of enrollment; 4) packaging of the course materials in a manner that they can be adapted by other colleges to meet local curriculum requirements; and 5) working with the colleges of the Virginia Community College System to develop a means for additional students to take the engineering, mathematics, and science courses that are not available on their campus.

The area of most concern being addressed in Phase II is to improve the collaborative learning activities and the computer systems on which they are based. It was found in Phase I in that voluntary collaboration in self-paced chemistry and mathematics courses was not sufficient to provide students access to peers or faculty. It was also found in the two engineering courses that required activities had to be positioned as central to the learning process in order for students and faculty to use the system for more than just the required activities. Lotus Notes™ was established as the computer conferencing system for the ALN, and its capability to record and accumulate student and faculty dialogue is a strength that can be built on. The complexity of the software, its relatively high support requirements, and projected costs are major problems. The lack of good drawing-input devices for home-study students and the inability to animate drawings are problems common to all computer conferencing systems.

Based on enrollments, the successful development of four complete home study courses, and the plans to refine the instructional model, ELI expects that with completion of Phase II, students will be able to communicate collaboratively through a robust ALN with each other and with faculty. More students will have access to an engineering degree and, as a result, because of the flexibility of home study, they will be able to take more courses per semester and be able to complete their degree in a shorter length of time.

Randal A. Lemke
Vice President of Education and Professional Development
International Communications Industries Association
11242 Waples Mill Road, Suite 200
Fairfax, VA 22030
(703) 273-7200
e-mail: rlemke@ziplink.net

Extended Learning Institute
Northern Virginia Community College
8333 Little River Turnpike
Annandale, VA 22003-3796
(703) 323-3379; fax: (703) 323-3392
e-mail: eli@nv.cc.va.us
URL: http://eli.nv.cc.va.us

Chapter 10

NORTHWESTERN MICHIGAN COLLEGE
Traverse City, Michigan

Ronda Edwards

Northwestern Michigan College (NMC) is a public community college located in Traverse City, Michigan, a rural resort area on the shores of Lake Michigan. Founded in 1951, the college is governed by a seven-member locally elected board of trustees. The college serves Grand Traverse County (population 64,273, the college's "district" and local tax base) and the four adjacent "service area" counties of Antrim, Benzie, Kalkaska, and Leelanau in northwestern lower Michigan. NMC also runs a branch campus in the city of Cadillac located in Wexford county, a community 50 miles south of Traverse City.

The region is considered a resort and retirement area in the state of Michigan. Two-thirds of all jobs are in the service industry. Northwestern Michigan College enrolled 3,937 students in the fall of 1995. Nearly 63 percent of these were part time, and 89 percent were enrolled in degree programs. The remaining 11 percent were enrolled to achieve job-related objectives or to satisfy personal interests. More than 9,000 additional students participate in noncredit continuing education offerings and customized training courses each year.

NMC introduced distance education opportunities in the winter of 1982 by offering a telecourse, "Focus on Society." Telecourses have been offered every year since, with an approximate annual enrollment of 175. In winter of 1993, the college embarked on another distance education venture—two-way instructional television courses to the branch campus in Cadillac. Positive reaction from both faculty and students prompted college officials to explore this option further. During 1986 through 1991, a number of studies, both formal and informal, suggested a keen interest in the expansion of baccalaureate and advanced degree programs for the citizens of northwestern Michigan.

In response to this need for expanded higher education opportunities, the Northwestern Michigan College Board of Trustees adopted the following goal in 1991–92: "To work in collaboration with other educational institutions to expand the baccalaureate, graduate, and continuing education options for area citizens while retaining the unique qualities of NMC as a comprehensive community college." In April of 1992, a group of 130 community leaders from Antrim, Benzie, Grand Traverse, Kalkaska, and Leelanau counties and the 15 school districts of the five-county area came together to discuss this goal. This "Founders 21 Committee" conducted an intense study of needs among the areas' populations—the general public, students, businesses, and potential educational partners—which culminated in a proposal for a "university center" to benefit all citizens of the region.

The university center concept is a partnership of Michigan universities, Northwestern Michigan College, the local public schools, and the communities of the five-county region to bring more baccalaureate and advanced degrees, continuing education, and high school curriculum enrichment to all residents of northwestern Michigan. In 1993, the president of NMC invited presidents of all four-year public and private institutions to submit programming proposals. NMC faculty committees approved 40 programs from 12 institutions (10 public and two private).

The NMC University Center/Project Interconnect Distance Education Network (NMCNet) is a hybrid system that connects two different video technologies together at the college. The University Center system employs compressed video technology utilizing Sprint phone lines to connect the University Center partner institutions to the college. The Project Interconnect network is an analog broadband system that connects the 15 local school districts in the five counties. At NMC, both systems are used (origination and reception), and connected as each application warrants.

Program Overview

Students Served and Programs Offered

While NMC is fulfilling its mission as an open-access comprehensive community college, most residents of northwestern Michigan nevertheless have been unable to continue their education beyond the associate's degree level. Major reasons for this problem include:

Geographic isolation. NMC is significantly isolated from four-year degree opportunities in the state of Michigan. The closest four-year school is 85 miles away.

Educational inequity. The 15 public universities of Michigan are supported annually by $1.3 billion in state tax dollars, of which the residents of northwestern Michigan contribute approximately $17.5 million—yet these four-year schools are available only to those who can leave the area.

Impediments to economic development. The most recent data shows per capita wages in the five counties are approximately 24 percent below the state average; attracting higher paying jobs to this region depends on enhancing higher education offerings.

Changing demographic profile. The average age of NMC students is 28. Sixty percent are female; one-third are single parents. Moreover, approximately 40 percent qualify for federal aid based on financial need. This profile reflects a population that is neither affluent nor mobile enough to move to the main campus of a university.

Limited professional development. Many employees in northwestern Michigan require additional education and/or certification to stay current or advance in their field, yet family and work responsibilities prevent them from leaving the area to seek this continuing education.

Dynamic area growth. The 1990 census indicates that between 1980 and 1990, 52 percent of the population growth in the state of Michigan occurred in the five-county northwestern Michigan region. The inability of residents to leave the area in search of higher education completion is a serious problem. Further, students in the region's small rural school districts lack the opportunity to experience a comprehensive high school curriculum due to the district's size and budgetary limitations. For area residents to achieve their potential educationally and economically, additional local higher education and curriculum enrichment opportunities were needed.

In response to these needs, the NMC University Center/Project Interconnect Network (NMCNet) was designed to accomplish the following:

- provide access to NMC courses and programs to residents in their local communities;
- provide access to four-year college and university courses and programs;
- provide access to advanced placement/dual enrollment instruction of college-level courses to K-12 students in their local schools;
- provide access to K-12 curriculum resource sharing and teacher education training at local school sites;
- and provide access to data transfer for instructional (Internet) and administrative uses.

Within the framework of the University Center, participating institutions have agreed to a partnership agreement which specifies that they will not provide any 100- or 200-level courses, and will waive all residency requirements for degrees. This agreement enhances the 2+2 educational opportunities from NMC. Faculty at NMC are involved in the preparation of curriculum for 2+2 programs and work with the universities to coordinate those curriculums.

Although NMC had been offering two-way instructional television courses to the students at the Cadillac site for three years, vastly expanded opportunities were made available with the inauguration of the NMC University Center and NMCNet in the fall of 1995. Within the network there are three separate and distinct activities: K-12 offerings, NMC courses, and University Center partner courses. In the first year, the K-12 system began by sharing a total of five courses among 10 school districts (Music Theory, French I, German I, Pre-Calculus, and Advanced Math). NMC offered six courses to its students at remote sites, including dual-enrollment options for high school seniors (US History to 1865, Western Civilization, Children's Literature, Japanese I, Contemporary Ethical Dilemmas, and Early Childhood Education). Finally, seven universities provided a total of 21 two-way interactive courses from their home campuses over the network.

Program Organization

The guiding principles of the University Center, including policies, procedures, responsibilities, and fees, are outlined in an 11-page document called a *Memorandum of Understanding.* The president of each participating institution and the president of NMC signed the *Memorandum.* Additionally, each president has assigned one representative to serve as liaison to the University Center. The liaisons meet as the Coordinating Committee with the University Center dean once each month.

Coordinating committee members designate institutional representatives to serve on seven task forces (Admissions/Academic Counseling, Financial Aid, Library, Marketing/Public Relations, Needs Assessment/ Evaluation, Noncredit Programs, and Technology). The task forces meet about two times each year. The chief academic officer from each participating university designates a representative to serve on a council to review program proposals and to deliberate on policy issues. As a grassroots initiative spearheaded by NMC, the University Center has relied on input, donations, and staff support from numerous groups and individuals in the five-county service area.

A 25-member University Center Advisory Committee, whose members were selected by the NMC president and University Center dean from the five counties, meets with the University Center dean quarterly to provide input in University Center programming and operations. The collaboration with the local K-12 school districts and the intermediate school district was an extension of existing agreements that codified facility usage and continues with ongoing discussion on collaboration in the areas of administrative software management, purchasing, and warehousing.

Each district agreed to a set of principles outlined in the *Consortium Partnership Agreement.* The agreement basically allows the college to use a classroom at each school district to house the network equipment. Each school district provided renovations to meet project specifications and use the network classroom during the school day for school activities. NMC has exclusive use of each classroom beginning at 4 p.m. each day and on the weekends. NMC provides dual-enrollment opportunities for each school district at their request, and professional development activities are shared among all participants.

The distance education program at NMC is a collaboration among administrative and academic divisions of the college and the local school districts through the coordination efforts of the Traverse Bay Area Intermediate School district, as well as the NMC University Center office and the University Center partner institutions. The distance education program at NMC is considered another delivery system used to facilitate the mission of the college of open access for all residents. The NMC Media Services Division provides technical support and is responsible for the construction and maintenance of the network(s). The division is also charged with providing the training and assistance needed by faculty to be effective educators over the network, as well as scheduling the courses requested.

The Media Services Division director reports to the vice president of Educational Services concerning matters of the distance education program. Support personnel for the program include a part-time faculty training coordinator, a full-time administrative assistant, a full-time instructional designer, two full-time technicians, and a technical coordinator who all report to the Media Services Division director. The division also hires and trains site facilitators for distant sites to assist the instructor.

Courses are scheduled as requested by the college academic divisions, the Cadillac branch campus, the school districts (for dual enrollment), and the University Center partner institutions.

NMC faculty teach on the network on a voluntary basis and are supported in this endeavor by the Media Services staff with training and individualized instructional development support. Faculty report to their academic divisions for all teaching, including the distance education program. Academic division directors communicate with the Media Services director regarding their instructors' progress on the interactive television network.

NMC faculty who elect to teach over the system are compensated for two course sections during the first semester of teaching on the network. During subsequent semesters, faculty pay is based on enrollment; compensation for students beyond the course maximum is paid on a prorated basis until the number of students equals another section. Faculty have the option of adding additional students beyond the original course maximum count. The local school districts or universities are responsible for the compensation of their faculty.

The construction of the networks and classrooms was funded with federal and local grants and donations. The distance education program was initially funded through a professional development grant from the Kellogg Foundation which paid for training and instructional development activities, as well as several staff members. The program will sustain its present base with user fees to universities who access their students through the network.

Instructional Strategies

Instruction over the network is predominately synchronous where instructors and students see and hear each other at the same time using television monitors. Instructors teach to a classroom in front of them (the origination site) and to a maximum of three additional sites (remote locations). One of the main objectives for instructors is to incorporate as much interactivity as possible, so that students at the remote sites do not shift into a passive phase of "watching TV." Teaching on the system is voluntary. NMC faculty who wish to do so are responsible for the development of their course and are assisted by the NMC Media Services Division in a variety of ways. Each instructor is required to participate in a training workshop that covers instructional techniques for being effective and successful on the system. Training topics include organization, involvement/interactivity, handouts, graphics, presentation skills, technology in the classroom, and logistics of the network. After completing the workshop, the instructor has the option of receiving assistance from an instructional designer. The faculty member and the instructional designer

work as a team to address such issues as "chunking" the content, sequencing activities, matching strategies with objectives, alternatives to lecture, ways to visualize tough concepts that don't seem visual, using interaction effectively, using more or different ways to engage learners and keep them active in the learning process, selecting and creating appropriate exercises or practices, and building good assessment tools.

Numerous strategies have been used by instructors to engage learners and humanize the distance-delivery system. Instructors interact with individual students by using *their* names, rather than by using a remote site name. Because this is a visual delivery medium, instructors also enhance their presentations with graphics, still images, videotapes, slides, and computer images. Faculty use small group discussion at all sites to encourage student to student interaction. Cross-site groups are also possible, so students likewise become involved with students at other sites. Students interact with the technology themselves, and become very comfortable with it. Faculty will often ask students to do presentations where students speak from the teacher's podium and control cameras, use graphics and maintain interactivity with the faculty and other students at all sites. Games or other activities which involve students across all sites are sometimes used.

Faculty are also trained to use alternative approaches such as multimedia and the Internet, allowing them to spend some of the class time involving students in thinking about the ideas and concepts presented, and reacting to and applying information. Faculty are also trained in techniques for information mapping, concept mapping (or word pictures), and guided note taking. All of these provide further support for students, alternative "channels" for the distribution of information, as well as ways to engage the students through working with the course content. Additional student/instructor interactivity is accomplished through phone and fax connections. Each NMC and University Center student is provided an e-mail address and account with the enrolling institution. Internet connections are used for student-instructor and student-student correspondence as well as to provide an alternative for dissemination of instruction or for student use in turning in assignments.

Technologies Employed

The NMC University Center/Project Interconnect Distance Education Network is a hybrid telecommunications system that provides high-quality two-way video and audio to specially equipped classrooms throughout the NMC service area and across the state to the University Center partners. The hybrid system combines digitized compressed video via Sprint T-1 phone lines and BTNA CODECs from University Center partner campuses and the analog CATV video network linking NMC with 15 local school districts throughout the area (Project Interconnect). The network also allows each location to connect to the Internet and to send faxes. The entire network is private and secured, which means that it cannot be viewed by others outside of the classroom viewing options. When NMC began looking at transmitting courses to the Cadillac campus in 1992, the decision was made to use digital video compression and take advantage of the newly created statewide network in Michigan which connects colleges and universities. This system employs the Sprint Video Network Services and provides low transmission costs via T-1 phone lines. The decision to use fiber for the system was based on several factors:

- The local cable company had installed fiber-optics cable for schools while upgrading their fiber plant. This presented an attractive alternative since the cost to local school districts and the college would be a minimal monthly access fee.
- The technology proposed for the video interaction portion of this project is a mature format—CATV, and can be easily interconnected with the compressed digital video format.

Within NMCNet, the college houses the hub that receives and distributes compressed video signals throughout the NMC campus and the analog CATV system. The digital compressed video signals are received from the partner universities and sent via the college's existing video distribution network to interactive classrooms on the main campus, the University Center campus (three miles southwest), and/or to any site in the analog CATV system utilizing a routing switcher. In order to allow multiple sites to be seen and heard on the far end of the compressed video site, a bridge switching system is used.

The two-way interactive television classroom design was based on research findings from other systems as identified in *Linking for Learning*, NMC instructor input, and specifications from the Michigan Collegiate Telecommunications Association (MiCTA). The classrooms include four cameras (teacher, student, document, and fixed room), monitors for student and instructor viewing, microphones, an audio echo cancellation system, videotape player/recorder, auxiliary inputs for computers, laser disk players, slides, etc., and a software-based touch screen equipment integrator with the ability for far-end control of the cameras.

The classrooms are controlled by the instructor and do not require additional personnel for camera switching or audio monitoring. Each classroom also has a fax/copier for dissemination of handouts, tests, assignments, and other materials, as well as a phone for private conversations. The success of the students, both at the remote locations and at the origination site, is dependent on the teaching success of the faculty, technical expertise of staff, and the participation and commitment of the students. The use of instructional technology to enhance the learning process and to make distance education students an integral part of the instructional process requires specific skills. NMC has designed and is implementing a threefold approach to human resource development for the interactive television network, which includes development activities for faculty, for the administrators and technical staff at all locations, and for the students in the classrooms.

NMC has employed a faculty member who has several years of experience teaching over the system to conduct the specific training events for faculty, staff, and technical and site facilitators. The faculty training includes a two-day hands-on

training session covering specific instructional techniques for the interactive video classroom, such as maximizing interaction, humanizing the technology, developing presentation skills, visualizing the content, organizing and planning the course, handling copyright issues, and managing multiple sites. The training also includes time for individual presentations over the system to allow instructors to become familiar with the equipment controls. The training is followed by individualized course development with an instructional designer to reconstruct courses for presentation over the system. Additionally all faculty are able to participate in peer colleague dialog activities with colleagues at other institutions involved in distance education.

Staff and site facilitator training is given in a half-day session to provide these critical "first-line" personnel with accurate information which will enable them to assist all distance education classes. Items addressed in these sessions include systems operation, instructional interactivity, troubleshooting procedures, and hands-on experience with the technology. Faculty and staff from the K-12 systems and the University Center partner institutions also participate in the NMC training. This is another example of the cooperation and collaboration among the three distinct users of NMCNet.

Student Services Provided

To ensure that the student has an optimal experience as a "distant" learner at a remote site classroom, an orientation video program was produced and is shown at the beginning of each course. This program acquaints the student with the unique features of this type of instruction, including what technologies are used in the classroom, how the student can interact with the instructor, what to do if technical difficulties arise at the remote site, and how to make the best use of this teaching strategy. NMC students register for distance education courses utilizing the college telephone registration system. University Center students register at the NMC University Center in Traverse City. Text and course materials can be purchased at the college bookstore or sent to the remote sites for dissemination.

Learning resources are accessed using the connections to the main NMC library and/or other university libraries. The network can also be accessed for student questions on administrative issues. The NMC Counseling Department is utilizing the video network to provide academic advising, testing, as well as student orientation and other student services to potential students throughout the network. Local high school counselors assist the college as site facilitators at their locations by marketing the service to seniors, proctoring tests, and assisting with college orientation.

Student Grading and Program Evaluation:

There are no significant differences between the measurement of student progress in regular classes and within the new program. Faculty assess all students in the same manner, and, at the remote sites, facilitators assist the faculty in assessments. The college's experience with distance education reflects the national trend that students at remote sites progress as well or better than students at the origination site.

Program assessment is done with every class each semester. A survey is specifically constructed to elicit comments and concerns regarding the students' experience on the network. The surveys are reviewed by the Media Services director, the Technical Coordinator and the Faculty Training Coordinator, who assess any necessary changes to the classroom, network, and/or training workshops. Faculty are asked for their input, which is used to redesign, fine tune, or add to the two-way interactive television classrooms, or any other aspect of the distance education program and services.

Unique or Exemplary Practices

The network is an excellent example of cooperation and collaboration among 15 K-12 systems, a community college, and 12 four-year institutions. There are a variety of programming components. Within Project Interconnect, each of the 15 school districts uses the network for shared courses and professional development activities. Within the University Center system, those partner institutions offer courses to NMC students and continuing education to community members. NMC uses both systems to provide greater access to educational opportunities for all residents in the service district.

The uniqueness of the NMCNet is collaboration. NMC is the connecting link between each program, and provides training and technical expertise to the entire network. The uniqueness is the semi-decentralized structure of the network administration. Operating costs are lowered because there is no large central administrative staff. All administrative concerns for the K-12 system are referred to the intermediate school district, and within the University Center issues are referred to the dean of the University Center. The collaborative spirit among all the participating educational institutions is the reason why it works.

Ronda Edwards
Director, Media & Distance Education Services
Northwest Michigan College
1701 East Front Street
Traverse City, MI 49686
(616) 922-1075; fax: (616) 922-1080
e-mail: redwards@nmc.edu

Chapter 11

RIO SALADO COLLEGE
Tempe, Arizona

Patricia S. Case and Charlcey Brabec

Rio Salado College is one of 10 colleges and centers in the Maricopa County Community College District (MCCCD) located in Maricopa County, Arizona. The MCCCD is the second largest community college district in the United States, and serves more than 125,000 students each year.

Maricopa County is larger than the state of Maryland, with high-density urban areas and low-density, isolated rural areas. In order to serve the 9,226 square miles of Maricopa County, Rio Salado College was established in 1978 as a "College Without Walls." Rio Salado was designated as the nontraditional college for the district, providing instruction with primarily part-time, adjunct faculty in rented or leased facilities to more than 27,000 college-credit students, 10,000 noncredit students, and more than 100 businesses, not only in Arizona but throughout the United States.

Rio Salado has been meeting the postsecondary educational needs of special populations throughout Maricopa County since 1978, emphasizing educational efforts with high-risk youth, first generation college students, adult learners, those with English language literacy needs, and residents of underserved or isolated geographic areas. Rio Salado has consistently focused on quick delivery and custom-designed educational services, and was created to adapt to community and demographic changes quickly and efficiently and to meet the needs of a changing population and a changing business community.

In the 1994–95 fiscal year, Rio Salado served over 20,000 credit students (unduplicated head count) throughout Maricopa County. In addition, the college provided basic skills programs for 14,000 noncredit students.

Rio Salado is proud of its record of educational service delivery. In the 1995–96 school year, students will take courses at approximately 250 sites and more than 5,900 students will receive in-home instruction through distance education. Given the rapid population growth in Arizona and the types of new businesses locating within the state, the need for a better-educated work force will be greater than ever, and Rio Salado is meeting those needs increasingly through distance education.

Program Overview

When Rio Salado was founded, one of the designated programs assigned to the college was distance education. With a wide range of courses leading to an associate's degree, Rio Salado's distance education program now serves the diverse needs of the over two million Maricopa County residents.

Students Served and Programs Offered

The profile of the distance learner parallels that of the "typical" Rio Salado student regardless of program. The majority of students at Rio Salado are between the ages of 24 and 40, working full-time (53 percent), female (61 percent), single head of household (42 percent), with children and a high school education. To serve this particular customer base, Rio Salado built its programs to go beyond traditional college boundaries. Over 53 percent of entering Rio Salado students are new students to the system each semester. The vast majority are enrolled part-time. The number of female, single-parent students, older students, and employed students will continue to increase. In order to meet the educational requirements of these students, and to retain these students within the system, Rio Salado is continuing to expand its flexibility in course delivery.

Students are attracted to Rio Salado's distance education program for a variety of reasons, such as work schedule, parental responsibilities, physical needs of the home-bound, or to meet course requirements of the program. The program appeals to students who want to control their own pace or to choose the delivery system most appropriate for their learning style.

Course and Degrees

Rio Salado's distance education program can deliver over 70 courses, but in any given semester approximately 55 courses are offered. This range is sufficient for students who want to receive an associate of arts degree or to take courses leading to certificates in the areas of business and management. Rio Salado's offerings complement any degree-seeking student's program of work because all course offerings are student centered and competency based. Courses are equivalent to on-campus classes in content, assignments, and credits earned.

Program Organization

Distance education programs are housed within the Information Technologies Division of the college, headed by a dean of technology. The administrative responsibilities for the program are managed by a coordinator, who is assisted by two administrative staff, eight support staff, and four part-time employees. No faculty are assigned directly to the program; 13 full-time faculty at Rio Salado, however, contribute greatly to the development and success of the program by developing course materials, teaching courses, and developing student support services. The majority of the courses are taught by adjunct faculty who are proven master teachers in the classroom. Working with the full-time faculty, these instructors strive to ensure the success of each student. Faculty compensation is commensurate with the traditional classroom instructor pay, although the student/teacher ratio is somewhat higher for the distance education instructor.

The distance education program is funded in the same manner as traditional programs and has no special sources of funding.

Instructional Strategies

Rio Salado's approach to distance education is predominantly asynchronous. The primary strategies are:

Audiocassette. These courses are similar to print classes, but include supplementary information on cassette tapes to help the students with their studies. Students read the text and course guide as well as listen to additional information provided by the instructor or subject experts. The tapes are mailed to the student at no additional cost.

Online Computer. Students use a modem to connect their own computer to the college's mainframe computer to access assignments, fellow students, and the instructor. Students may take any course offered using the college's computer labs, or their own computer at home or at work; this method of delivery is known as the "Lab Without Walls." Special informative orientations are held for these kinds of courses.

World Wide Web. Faculty are currently developing a range of courses to be delivered via the World Wide Web. Students will access courses via their own online provider. These courses will be supplemented with textbooks, as well as audio and/or video materials.

Print-Based. These classes allow students to complete assignments during their own weekly time schedule. Instruction is provided through textbooks, study guides, and written communications from the instructor. Teleconference sessions are available for some classes.

Television. "Let your VCR go to class for you!" This is a popular option with many Rio Salado distance students. A wide variety of Rio Salado courses are broadcast every semester on the public educational channel (and some educational cable channels); students take classes in the comfort of their own home. If they miss a lesson, they may reserve a tape of that lesson through Rio's Library/Media Department.

Videocassette. In addition to printed material, a "lecture" portion of some classes is provided to students on videotapes, which they watch at their convenience. The use of visual images is intended to help students more easily understand difficult concepts. Videotapes are mailed to the student from the college.

These instructional strategies constitute 80 percent of the enrollments generated through distance education. The remaining distance education strategies employ synchronous methods:

Conference Call with Image Net. This delivery combines video computer graphics with two-way audio communication. Students use a modem to connect their own computer to the college's mainframe computer and have access to assignments, fellow students, and the instructor. Students without their own computers may take these classes from any of Rio's computer lab sites.

Telephone Conference Call Classes. These classes are "live" interactive sessions connecting students from many locations by telephone. The instructor and students become a "universal" class brought together by telephone lines. They may even take the class from their own phone or from a conference site. Conference call classes have even linked Rio students with students from other countries.

Video Conference Network. Students, separated by location, can join together with each other and their instructor by video technology, with cameras and monitors. A special "pad camera" allows visual images to be viewed in a full-screen format.

Mixed Media Courses. These courses use two-way conference calls and/or in-person meetings in combination with print materials, audiocassettes, videocassettes, or lab kit materials.

Faculty chairs are primarily responsible for the development of instructional materials. Course selection is based on meeting the needs of students in achieving an associate's degree, or specific certificate programs.

Technologies Employed

Maricopa's SUNDIAL Network contains a telephone bridge, the Image Net, and the Video Conferencing Network (VCN). The telephone bridge is used not only for the delivery of Rio Salado's distance-delivery courses but also for districtwide efforts. A coordinator and bridge operators maintain and operate this equipment.

The Media Department, in addition to meeting media needs collegewide, is responsible for all master tapes and provides tape duplication services. Within the media department, a graphics technician and audio-visual technician create the limited number of materials originated by the college. Most of the audio and videocassettes used in the program are leased through major providers. The library is responsible for processing all of these materials, cataloging, and check-in/check-out services.

A faculty messaging service allows students to leave private messages for instructors 24 hours a day. All messages are retrieved by the instructor within 24 to 48 hours.

The telephone is the instrument of choice to purchase all course materials; students may pick up materials or choose to have them delivered by mail. Rio Salado students may use the library services of any of the other nine Maricopa colleges. An electronic library is currently under development.

Although the majority of all Rio Salado students are advised via telephone, face-to-face appointments may be made at four strategic locations in the county. The initial contact for requesting tutoring is via the telephone; a tutoring coordinator then arranges for tutoring at a site and time convenient to the student. Student Services provides a 24-hour, 7-day tutor hotline in specific courses such as math and Spanish.

Counseling services are provided to students in several forms: individual and career counseling may be accessed by the student in person at four locations in the county or via telephone; computer counseling is offered to students taking computer courses; and a telephone outreach program targeting first-time distance education students has been operating for the past three years. The results of these interventions has significantly increased retention and improved grades for distance education students.

Student Grading and Program Evaluation

All courses have weekly assignments that are delivered to instructors via mail, fax, or computer by a date specified in the syllabus. The instructors grade and provide feedback on each assignment in a timely manner. With few exceptions, all students in this program are required to take a midterm and final exam in person. If students are unable to take a test on the designated date, they may arrange for an alternative date and time. Student Services coordinates testing for special-needs students. This approach to testing maintains the integrity and quality of the program.

Students evaluate courses and instructors each semester and feedback is given to the instructors. Instructors are also evaluated by their faculty chair. Because the success of the program is dependent on the adjunct instructor, a strong emphasis has been placed on mentoring and developing these valued employees. Many adjunct instructors have taught in the program for several semesters.

Unique or Exemplary Practices

A unique feature of Rio Salado's distance education program is Flex Start, a pilot program begun in the summer of 1995. In Flex Start, students begin selected classes on six consecutive Mondays and must complete courses within the traditional 13-week format. The response was overwhelmingly favorable for the pilot. The students liked being able to make choices about start dates and dates of completion. The favorable response from students indicated they felt in control of their schedule and more responsible for their educational programs. Key to the success of Flex Start was a concomitant flexible testing schedule. Fewer withdrawals occurred than in other distance education formats. Enrollment almost doubled in the summer of 1995 (1550 students) versus the summer of 1994 (820 students). Because of the success of Flex Start, it was incorporated in the spring 1996 schedule.

A second exemplary program is Rio Salado College's "Lab Without Walls," which offers computer courses throughout Maricopa County. Students with access to compatible computers and software can take these convenient, self-paced computer courses from their homes or offices. Everything from registration to taking the final exam can be done from their home or office. Troubleshooting support is provided by phone. Students are also eligible to use one of the four Rio Salado computer lab sites.

A third unique feature of Rio Salado's distance education program is a "Telephone Program for Student Empowerment" developed by a counseling faculty member and the director of student services. This outreach program is based on research

indicating that telephone contact has a positive effect on the retention of traditional and nontraditional college students. Similar research suggests that the more connected a student feels to an educational institution, the more likely they will be retained within a semester and persist between semesters. In this outreach program, students receive telephone calls from a counselor, counseling intern, or program advisor. The initial pilot, conducted in the spring semester of 1993, targeted courses with high dropout rates such as math and English. Since the pilot, a model has been developed that allows callers to identify those students most at-risk of not completing their course(s). The program was designed so that high-risk students receive several calls throughout the semester, compared to the two calls those in the lowest-risk category receive.

The first call is made at the beginning of the course to welcome students and to make sure they are on track. A second call is made at the end of the course to assist students in identifying their next course. Moderately at-risk students receive an additional call just before midterms to ensure that they are ready for the exam.

The highly at-risk student receives two additional calls. One call, just before the first assignment due date, encourages the student to complete assignments on time. The other additional call, approximately two weeks after the midterm, reassures and encourages students who may not have done as well as they would have liked. Overall, the program has had a positive effect on student retention in the distance education program. For example, first-time, female distance education students receiving two to four contacts showed an 85-percent retention rate, and math students had an overall retention rate of 83 percent. These retention rates surpass the rates districtwide for traditional classes.

Rio Salado's distance education program is committed to continuous improvement. It is a fluid, ever-changing, and growing partner in the growth of the college and the community.

Patricia S. Case
Faculty President & Faculty Chair for Sociology
Rio Salado College
2323 W. 14th Street
Tempe, AZ 85281
(602) 517-8264; fax: (602) 517-8259
e-mail: case@rio.maricopa.edu
URL: http://www.rio.maricopa.edu

Charlcey Brabec, Coordinator,
Educational Programs for Information Technologies
Rio Salado College
2323 W. 14th Street
Tempe, AZ 85281
(602) 517-8235; fax: (602) 517-8259
e-mail: brabec@rio.maricopa.edu

Chapter 12

SAN DIEGO CITY COLLEGE
San Diego, California

Curtis J. McCarty

Telecourses began in San Diego in 1968 with an experimental offering of one geology course in cooperation with KOGO-TV (now KGTV, Channel 10). Between 1969 and 1974, several TV courses in cultural studies, real estate, and property management were produced in cooperation with Channel 10. Additional offerings were introduced when the district joined in the nationwide "Sunrise Semester" program on the CBS network in 1972.

In 1973, a Committee on Alternative Delivery Instructional Systems was established as a sub-committee of the San Diego and Imperial Counties Community College Association. This resulted in a cooperative offering of telecourses on a consortium basis in the fall of 1974. The program's scope was enlarged to permit the offering of 14 TV courses during the 1976–77 year with an enrollment of nearly 1,000 students. In the early 1980s, however, as a result of the passing of Proposition 13, an educational funding restriction, and statewide fiscal uncertainties, several consortium districts, including San Diego, chose not to continue their participation. This led to the gradual reduction and ultimate termination of the program.

The district's most recent effort at distance education began in spring 1994. Reasons for the previous lack of progress were researched extensively and processes established to head off a recurrence of those earlier problems. Since then, the program has grown from six courses to eleven (Cultural Anthropology, Astronomy, Intro to Business, Business Law, Business Math, Child Development, Computer & Info Sciences, Geology 100, Intro to Photography, Psychology 101, and Spanish 101) and enrollments have been strong.

Program Overview

Students Served and Programs Offered

Since the fall term of 1994, 659 students have completed one or more distance education classes. Approximately 76 percent were female, mostly mothers with child-care concerns. Seventeen percent were African American, 40 percent Caucasian, and 14 percent Hispanic. An additional fifteen percent of these students belonged to other ethnic groups, and 15 percent went unreported.

The major reasons students said they enrolled in San Diego's distance learning courses were 1) the ability to stay at home with children; 2) convenience; 3) flexibility; 4) time saved; and 5) independence. The majority of students, when asked if they would take another distance education class, responded positively. The most gratifying responses have been consistent comments about how much students appreciate these offerings, the hope that they will continue, and questions about how soon other courses will be offered.

Program Organization

Distance education is offered throughout the district and is designed, organized, and maintained at San Diego City College, where it is administratively placed under the dean of learning resources. A faculty coordinator handles day-to-day operations and provides a link between the campus and the program. The operational philosophy places an emphasis on ensuring that communication lines remain open. As a result, regular channels between teaching faculty and the coordinator keep everyone informed about schedules, procedures, opportunities, and anything else that could prove helpful.

The program was designed to work within existing structures at the college; normal departmental and school procedures are followed. Faculty participate as a part of their regular load and reporting relationships (department chair and school deans) are not changed. Teaching staff are selected from several campuses through the district. One full-time contract faculty coordinator is supported by the City campus.

Instructional Strategies

Most current telecourses are obtained from InTeleCom (Intelligent Telecommunications), a nonprofit corporation and respected producer of television-based college-credit courses, including *The Mechanical Universe*, *Portrait of a Family*, and *Business and The Law*. As a consortium member, the district may use any of the 33 telecourses developed or held by InTeleCom. (The only current exception is the telecourse *Destinos* which is available from PBS Adult Learning Services.)

Initially, once faculty members express interest in a new distance learning course, the telecourse offerings from InTeleCom and other providers are reviewed. When an initial selection is made, a departmental curriculum review is made which confirms that the telecourse's curricula is a match for that of the traditional classroom course.

Each telecourse integrates at least one telecommunications medium (primarily video, but also others) with print materials to create a comprehensive learning experience. Telecourse offerings generally include the following components: 1) 26 to 30 half-hour video programs; 2) a textbook complementing the media instruction; 3) a student study guide integrating course components; and 4) a faculty manual containing a course syllabus, implementation strategies, a validated test bank, and promotional materials.

Video and print support materials are provided by InTeleCom. Course outlines are prepared by faculty members and submitted to the campus curriculum committee to ensure that campus communications remain open and that other faculty are kept informed.

The teacher is given a support packet of materials describing what happens in the video programs, and in what sequence. A contact with a experienced distance education teacher is suggested to help with any details as planning continues. A set of programs is loaned to the instructor to familiarize him or her with the materials as the course outline is prepared. In addition, the new teacher is kept informed of any changes to the program to help with preparation.

Typically, telecourse segments are broadcast twice weekly via cable and open circuit. If a student misses both the original broadcast and any repeats, back-up copies of each program are available for viewing (but not check-out) in the Learning Centers at the three main campuses. In addition, a company called RMI Media Productions, Inc. will rent (for a nominal charge) a complete set of videotapes to any student enrolled in the course. This arrangement is between the company and the student.

Since California law requires 48 contact hours for a "typical" three-unit course, and since the telecourse programs usually account for only 26 hours, the remaining 22 hours are conducted in a classroom setting. These 22 hours are prepared and delivered in a traditional classroom session by the faculty member.

Student Services Provided

San Diego's distance education program is conducted as nearly as possible like any other campus program. Students must enroll in the college and pay the same fees for the same number of units as any other student. As enrolled students, they have access to the same services (advisement, bookstore, health services, disabled student services, library, learning centers, and more) as any other student. The full range of services is available to all students.

Student Grading and Program Evaluation

Each course has a syllabus and a course outline that includes instructional goals and objectives, attendance requirements, grading criteria and procedures, a description of processes to achieve academic redress, and a schedule of topics. Teaching faculty are responsible for the maintenance of instructional activities (attendance records, performance evaluation, and assessment) in their respective classrooms, in the same manner as with traditional classes.

Overall effectiveness of the program is measured each semester by the faculty coordinator. At the first class meeting, demographic data, opinions, and perceptions about several distance education issues, reasons for taking a course by distance education versus a typical classroom experience; expectations of the course; and suggestions for additional courses are collected. At the semester's end, a final report is assembled based on the student's experiences from the beginning of the course. The report reviews students' before and after responses to the distance education experience, comparing, among other things, the expected grade to the one received, the expected degree of difficulty between this and other courses, reasons for taking the course, and comments or suggestions for change. As a result of data from these surveys, the non-TV part of the courses have often been changed, additional courses have been offered, and new telecourses are being planned for the future.

This information is also sent to InTeleCom for their review. Telecourse enrollments are strong and supported by campus advertising, mailings, and student word-of-mouth advertising. Retention percentages compare favorably with the general district figures. Recently, based on the successes just described, program funding was renewed for another year.

Unique or Exemplary Practices

The uniqueness of this approach is in its difference from previous efforts to establish a distance education curriculum at the district. Wide-based faculty support was elicited so that all levels of the organization would be involved in the decision. The program was purposefully developed slowly, and the entire process was kept open so that anybody wanting information (good and bad) would have access.

Faculty expressed interest in participation, but were concerned about how compensation was to be determined; 70 percent thought it would be a good way to reach more students or those who hadn't been reached thus far. Of the individual faculty comments, all dealt with details of how the course would be offered, how these courses would be accommodated into current curricula, or whether these courses would be accepted by or transfer into other colleges. Most were positive statements of support for the distance education concept provided normal curricular procedures were followed.

College faculty have been supportive because participation has been strictly voluntary. Since distance education has been considered an innovation, those who might become involved have to be able to get information about it, try it out on a small scale, and be convinced that it is beneficial and has support. So far, those who have tried the program have stayed on. At each step in the process, the major constituents were encouraged and allowed to "buy in" so that no one felt the project was being railroaded.

Because of this base level of commitment, the program has fared well. The rancor experienced by other programs that were designed and built "behind closed doors" or without direct involvement of the professional staff has been avoided. As yet, no degree programs are being offered via distance education, but it seems clear that there will be degree programs once the college community becomes totally committed to distance education as a complement to classroom participation. The program is bound to grow and provide an even greater range of services to students.

Curtis J. McCarty
Faculty Coordinator, Distance Education
San Diego City College
1313 Twelfth Avenue
San Diego, CA 92101-4787
(619) 230-2534; fax (619) 230-2063
e-mail: cmcarty@sdccd.cc.ca.us

Chapter 13

SINCLAIR COMMUNITY COLLEGE
Dayton, Ohio

Peggy Falkenstein

Sinclair Community College is a comprehensive two-year public institution that offers a wide range of educational opportunities and services to meet the needs of the citizens of the Miami Valley and the state of Ohio. In existence for over 100 years, the college serves nearly 21,000 students. Sinclair is the largest of the Dayton area's seven institutions of higher education, accounting for a third of the local enrollment. It is also among the 20 largest single campus community colleges in the nation with over 1,400 different credit courses in 101 academic disciplines offering 46 associate's degrees in 25 areas of emphasis. As a comprehensive institution, Sinclair not only prepares students for transfer into upper division baccalaureate programs at universities and for initial entry into technical careers, but also offers extensive opportunities to update technical knowledge needed in today's global economy.

Program Overview

In order to provide greater access to education for the people in its service area, Sinclair added a distance learning program to its curricular offerings in 1979. During the first year, preproduced telecourses were licensed and offered over public television. Then, through a special request from a commercial television station in need of public service programming, the college began developing and producing its own telecourses. Using the studio and production facilities of the county joint vocational high school, two telecourses were produced and offered for credit over this commercial television station in 1980.

The uniqueness of the Sinclair distance learning program centers around these in-house productions. Telecourses are scripted and recorded by both full- and part-time Sinclair faculty. Using computer generated graphics, electronic white boards, video floppy players, and other enhancements—and occasionally supplementing lectures with demonstrations or interviews with local guest experts—these telecourses provide distant students with the same course content as campus students, but with greater convenience and flexibility.

Good enrollment and positive feedback generated from the first two internally produced courses convinced the administration that telecourses were meeting a local need for education. As a result, Sinclair continued to produce its own telecourses, adding four to six new courses each year and, at the same time, licensing externally produced telecourses as needed. Currently, over 70 different courses are available on a regular basis with more than 2,000 enrollments per quarter and over 7,500 enrollments annually. For the past five years,

Sinclair has lead all colleges and universities in the state of Ohio in enrollments in distance learning courses.

For the first 10 years, the distance learning program consisted primarily of telecourses with student-instructor interaction occurring by means of telephone, mail, fax, and appointments. This being a somewhat passive form of delivery, another component was added to bring about greater interactivity not only between student and instructor but among the students themselves.

By means of the Dayton Area Freenet (DAFN), and using a combination of message boards and read-only screens, students with computers and modems were able to access important course information online, discuss topics with other students, and communicate with their instructors. This became known as the Sinclair Electronic College (SEC). The major course content was still taped telecourses, but the computer provided an additional enhancement to the program.

Finally, in the fall of 1995, Sinclair began offering "live" interactive courses via an ITFS delivery system (one-way video, two-way audio). Starting with five remote sites at high schools within a 25-mile radius, the college offered several courses after school and in the evening. Additional courses, workshops, and training sessions will be added as the college expands the system to include businesses, hospitals, and other organizations. As a result of partnering with a wireless cable company, these courses can also be made available to individuals in their homes. This "live" delivery system has been termed LEARNing Works and is a joint effort of Sinclair Community College, Wright State University, and Greater Dayton Public Television.

Since the college is committed through its mission and philosophy to meeting the needs of the Miami Valley Community by providing greater access to education and training and by keeping education affordable, plans are in place to continue to grow the distance learning program. An associate of arts degree, transferable to a four-year institution, is currently available. Additional degree programs will be added. As its emphasis shifts from teaching to learning, the college continually explores alternatives that will meet student needs and student learning styles and will continue to be a leader in these endeavors.

Students Served and Programs Offered

The Distance Learning Program provides alternatives to the traditional classroom setting for individuals with scheduling conflicts or family and work commitments, who are homebound, live a distance away from the campus, or who merely prefer to study independently. The typical community college student is the older adult learner who is returning to school to get a degree, to update skills, to take courses toward a promotion, or to maintain certification. The distance learner is no different. The average age of the Sinclair distance learner is 31. Seventy-three percent are female.

These individuals cannot afford to wait eight or 10 years to accomplish their goals. If a campus course is not available at the time or day or quarter it is needed, this presents a major roadblock for them and they seek alternatives to meet their educational needs. Usually such individuals are self-directed and motivated enough to handle independent study successfully. Surveys conducted among Sinclair students show that approximately 80 percent are combining campus courses with distance learning courses to obtain degrees or update their skills in a more timely manner. Courses in the distance learning program are taken by many in the community for personal enrichment. Senior citizens find this a convenient way to pursue the educational interests that may not have been available to them when they were younger.

Telecourses are the largest component of the distance learning program. These courses are offered over public television, on five cable channels, over an ITFS system, and through an extensive check-out program. The check-out program is the most popular way that students access the telecourses. They find it more convenient to have the videotapes available for viewing as their schedule permits. Students check out the videotapes for the entire course at the start of the quarter and must return them at the end of the quarter. There is no cost to the student unless the videotapes are returned after the deadline (the last day of the quarter). In such cases, a late fee is assessed.

Telecourses are available in each of the six academic divisions: Allied Health, Business Technologies, Engineering Technologies, Extended Learning, Fine and Performing Arts, and Liberal Arts, but, the majority of the telecourses are from the business technologies and liberal arts areas. Over 20 disciplines within the six divisions are represented in the telecourses offerings: allied health, business ownership, computer information systems, economics, law, management, marketing, office information systems, automotive technology, quality engineering technology, experienced-based education, developmental studies, law enforcement, art appreciation, art history, communications, music, astronomy, English, geology, history, literature, physics, philosophy, psychology, and sociology.

While most telecourses address student needs for basic introductory courses in the various disciplines, they also allow departments to offer some specialized courses that are required in a particular program but which do not generate enough enrollments to warrant multiple sections or continual offering each quarter. Frequently, department chairs face such a dilemma regarding certain courses: if a course section is offered both day and evening, neither section draws enough enrollment to make it cost effective. Regardless of the decision made between a day or an evening section, some students will suffer due to scheduling conflicts. By offering such a course in a telecourse mode, it can be available to any student during any quarter.

Telecourses have also become a way to offer a "special topics" course or to introduce a new course into a department's curriculum to ascertain interest and need. Again, courses of this nature are risky in a classroom environment that relies on numbers in order to be cost effective.

Courses offered through the distance learning program parallel those offered in the classroom, giving students a choice of either format. There are few "elective" courses, however, that are available only as telecourses, and others that are offered some terms only as distance learning options and other terms in both formats. Telecourses carry the same academic credit, have the same course objectives, and provide the same transferability as classroom courses.

Students are able to complete an associate of arts degree through the distance learning program by combining these telecourses, the electronic college courses, the "live" interactive courses, and independent-study courses. Plans are underway to extend this option to students pursuing a business technology degree.

Program Organization

The distance learning program is an academic division under the vice president for instruction and is administered by the dean of distance learning. In addition, a full-time professional position—the coordinator of distance delivery—reports to the dean. Finally, there are two secretarial positions: secretary to the dean and secretary for the distance learning program.

The Distance Learning division houses the taped telecourse program known as TV Sinclair, the computer-delivered instruction known as the Sinclair Electronic College, the "live" interactive course delivery via ITFS known as LEARNing Works (Lifelong Education And Resource Network), and satellite uplinking and downlinking resources.

With the recent reorganization of the Continuing Education Department, all off-campus, in-person courses are now part of the Distance Learning Division. This includes several area high school satellite sites, Wright Patterson Air Force Base, Defense Electronics and Supply Corporation, and the Dayton Correctional Institution.

Faculty (both full- and part-time) from various departments and divisions work closely with the dean and the coordinator of distance learning in developing and managing courses within the distance learning program, but they remain housed within their discipline and report directly to their department chairs. They are responsible, however, for providing the distance learning office with all syllabi, handouts, and other information needed by the students. The distance learning office provides support to the faculty by distributing all materials to students, including test results and graded assignments.

All testing for taped telecourses is done on campus. Faculty determine the number of tests to be given for each course and are required to provide a group testing time and make-up testing as needed. To provide more convenience and flexibility for students and faculty, a testing center is available on campus for make-up tests. The use of this testing facility is up to the discretion of the individual faculty member.

Faculty are compensated both for course development and

course management. Because of the time and effort involved in the planning and preparation of internally produced courses, faculty members are given five credit hours compensation for developing and recording a telecourse. The compensation is the same for faculty who prepare and teach a "live" interactive course for the first time. If a telecourse is externally licensed, faculty members receive 2.5 credit hours compensation for reviewing the videotapes and accompanying manuals and preparing course materials for students. Compensation for either type of telecourse preparation can be taken as overload pay or as reassigned time. Many faculty take the reassigned time to reduce their teaching load while preparing the course.

When a telecourse is offered in any given term, faculty are compensated on a per student enrollment basis. For a three-credit-hour course (which most of the telecourses are) a tenth of a credit hour (.1) is awarded per student enrolled up to 40 students. After 40, the compensation drops to .075 credit hours per student. Pay adjustments are made upward for four- and five-credit-hour telecourses (1.25 credit hours up to 40 students; one credit hour for 40 and above) as well as downward for one- and two-credit-hour courses (.075 credit hours for up to 40 students; .050 credit hours for 40 and above).

Students pay the same amount of tuition for distance learning courses as for on-campus courses. No additional fees are charged. Tapes loaned to students through the "check-out" program are free, but a late fee is charged if the tapes are not returned on time. The student must incur the cost of tape replacement if tapes are damaged or lost.

Videotapes in the tape check-out program, syllabi, and other handouts are distributed on campus at the start of every term from the Individualized Learning Center, an independent-study lab which houses VCRs, computers, and other technologies for student usage. A bar coding system is used for tracking the videotapes. After several years of providing this service for students, it has proven to be very effective and beneficial. There is minimal loss and damage. Each term, over 1,500 sets of tapes are distributed. While three to four percent may be returned late in a given term, less than one percent have not been returned at all over this time period.

Instructional Strategies

The distance learning program employs three main instructional strategies: pretaped telecourses, computer-based asynchronous courses, and "live" interactive, one-way video, two-way audio courses.

The pretaped telecourses, both internally produced and externally licensed, are delivered to students over public television, cable, and ITFS. They are also available on videotapes for taking home. In addition, all telecourses are housed in the Individualized Learning Center (ILC) where students can access them for on-campus viewing as needed.

Computer-based courses are accessed via the Dayton Area Freenet. At the start of each quarter, students enrolled in these courses are provided with an ID and password and must attend a required orientation session. Since the public freenet telephone numbers are frequently used, Sinclair

students and faculty are provided with a special telephone connection through a UNIX server on campus. Most students use their own computers and modems from home, but computers are available on campus in the ILC for students without home computers. Plans are underway to locate computers and modems at off-campus sites such as libraries, high schools, or government centers for greater access and convenience for students.

Since the primary intent of these computer-based courses is to promote interactivity between students and instructors and among students themselves, a series of bulletin boards has been established for this purpose. Each course can have as many discussion boards as desired by the instructor, but generally there are two. On one, the instructor may pose discussion questions, cite current events, or even play the devil's advocate to encourage interaction and promote critical thinking. The students themselves may also provide the questions. In some instances, instructors award points for participation. The other bulletin board allows for "anonymous" questioning by students who are reluctant to reveal their identity. In addition to the discussion boards in each course, there is also a "student union" bulletin board available through the main menu which allows for dialog among all students regardless of the course in which they are enrolled. Frequently the messages on this board tend to be more socially oriented rather than discipline oriented.

"Live" interactive courses are currently being delivered to remote sites at area high schools. Receive sites are equipped with a special antenna for receiving the programming. These courses are conducted simultaneously with an on-campus class. A site facilitator is employed at the remote locations to distribute materials, proctor tests, and facilitate communication between instructor and students.

Whether preparing a taped telecourse or one that is delivered "live," instructors have available to them an instructional design person, a graphic artist, and other faculty who have previously developed telecourses. Final decisions regarding the design of the course, the course content, and the organization, however, are left to the discretion of the instructor.

Technologies Employed

In both TV Sinclair courses and Sinclair Electronic College courses, the primary technologies employed are TVs, VCRs, and computers. These are supplemented with telephones and fax machines. The purpose of the computer-based courses is to promote interactivity among students and between student and instructor. However, since the freenet provides access to various databases, discussion groups, and other sources of information, students are encouraged to explore these to supplement their learning.

The "live" interactive courses employ a wide variety of technologies. The interactive classroom, from which these courses are taught, is equipped with a computer with CD-ROM, a laser disc player, ceiling-mounted video projector, video floppy player, CDI, video overhead, and VCR. Faculty are trained in the use of these technologies by the coordinator for distance delivery, who also assists faculty in incorporating technology into the instructional design of their courses. Faculty are encouraged to use as many technologies as needed in order to bring about greater interactivity and student involvement in the learning process. Students in the campus class also use the technologies available to do class presentations or other activities.

The Center For Interactive Learning lab (CIL) is equipped with a variety of technologies for experimentation and research. If an instructor wants to "learn" a new technology, review the content of a CD-ROM, do a video capture, or learn how to use the Internet before incorporating these into their courses, the CIL lab serves this purpose. The CIL lab is staffed with faculty mentors who serve as peer tutors to their colleagues.

Student Services Provided

Students register for all distance learning courses in the same manner as other campus students: via telephone, mail, or in person. Textbooks are available at the campus bookstore and other bookstores off campus. Because of the tremendous cost incurred with mailing, and since students are not assessed a fee for distance learning courses, students must come to campus to check out and return videotapes and access their syllabi. With proper ID and proof of course registration, these materials can also be picked up by someone designated to do so by the student. In a few instances, videotapes and syllabi have been mailed to the student if great distance or a disability prohibits that individual from coming onto the campus.

Students can access materials from the Sinclair campus Learning Resources Center (LRC), area public libraries, or other college and university libraries. Through a statewide computerized database system called OHIOLink, books, periodicals, journals, and other materials can be readily accessed and delivered within 24 hours from any library statewide.

In-person advising is primarily done on campus. Some academic advising, however, is provided at off-campus satellite centers at the start of registration for each term. Plans are underway to conduct advising "live" to remote sites via the LEARNing Works Network (ITFS) and through the Sinclair Electronic College.

In-person tutoring is provided on the campus and is available to all students free of charge. Distance learning students more commonly receive help with their coursework from their instructor via telephone and less often in person.

Recently, a student services videotape was developed to acquaint distance learning students with the various services available to them. The two-and-a-half minute tape describes each service area and gives campus locations and telephone numbers. The tape is bundled with all videotapes that are checked out and can be aired prior to courses broadcast on public television and cable. Additional student services videotapes are planned.

Student Grading and Program Evaluation

Grading and assessment are the domain of the individual instructor and department in which the telecourse is housed. However, testing or some other means of assessment is required for each course. All testing is done on campus.

Sinclair Community College has a very extensive assessment program in place throughout its campus in all disciplines and divisions. Each program has stated outcomes and standards by which those outcomes will be measured. Distance learning courses are subject to the same assessment processes as their campus counterparts.

Unique or Exemplary Practices

In most colleges, distance learning telecourses are licensed from external vendors and adapted to fit a particular curriculum offering. Licensed telecourses are accompanied by a faculty manual which serves to aid the faculty member in structuring the course components.

The Sinclair Community College Distance Learning Program is unique in that most of the telecourses have been internally produced. They are scripted and recorded by Sinclair full- and part-time faculty. These programs are primarily lecture based, and while they are not elaborate productions, they have served the college well.

The "in-house" productions fulfill a curriculum need in cases where no externally produced telecourses are available. They are very cost effective, provide for greater faculty "buy-in" (since faculty determine content), generate good enrollments, and provide a mechanism for offering required but low-enrollment courses

An even more unique situation is that Sinclair does not have its own production studio. From the beginning, these internally produced courses have been outsourced. Initially, Sinclair had an arrangement with the county vocational school for renting their production facilities. Producers and directors were hired on a part-time basis. More recently, however, Sinclair has been working with the local public television station in much the same capacity. Such arrangements have positive benefits: they are a good way of partnering with the community, and they have proven to be cost effective.

The in-house productions are beneficial to the college in other ways as well. In the early years especially, when distance learning was not as readily accepted and faculty buy-in was difficult to obtain, faculty were more receptive to considering a course they could develop themselves. Together with their department, they exercised control of the course content, format, and the finished product. Frequently, faculty resisted using externally produced telecourses because they had no control over content.

For many faculty, putting together a telecourse provides a means for creativity and innovation. Compensation in the form of reassigned time or overload pay is an additional incentive. Moreover, since the college has a well-structured and accepted promotion and merit system in place, telecourse development is one of the activities or accomplishments that can be submitted for consideration and is frequently recognized and rewarded.

One less obvious benefit of in-house telecourse production is the way the process itself makes faculty begin to rethink their course organization and presentation. Complacency can easily occur after years of teaching the same course in the same manner. Many faculty contend that developing telecourses has changed their classroom style and their attitude towards students.

Another unique feature of Sinclair's distance learning program, in addition to the in-house productions, is the extensive check-out program. This has been one of the major contributing factors to the tremendous enrollment growth. In spite of the fact that courses are offered on public television and local cable channels, the overwhelming preference of students is to check the videotapes out and take them home. Almost every telecourse offered is made available to students for checking out.

While viewed as a benefit by students, the size and scope of this service does create logistical challenges to the college. Problems such as storage, duplication, and inventory control are just a few. As the number of course offerings expand and enrollments increase, the distribution, management and retrieval of videotapes becomes a full-time concern.

Sinclair continues to search for ways to enhance its program. Video programs will be supplemented or eventually replaced by CD-ROM. Courses will be delivered via the Internet and the World Wide Web. And as technologies continue to abound, distance learning will serve as the vehicle to increase opportunities to better serve the educational needs of students.

Peggy Falkenstein
Dean, Distance Learning
Sinclair Community College
444 West Third Street
Dayton, OH 45402
(513) 449-6144; fax: (513) 226-2891
e-mail: pfalkens@sinclair.edu

Chapter 14

TARRANT COUNTY JUNIOR COLLEGE DISTRICT
Hurst, Texas

Kevin R. Eason and Carolyn C. Robertson

Formed in 1965, the Tarrant County Junior College District (TCJC) now encompasses three campuses with a fourth campus to open in fall 1996. The South Campus opened for classes in fall 1967, the Northeast Campus in the fall 1968, and the Northwest Campus in January 1976. The May Owen District Center, located in downtown Fort Worth, houses the district and community campus offices and opened in March 1983. The Southeast Campus, located in Southeast Arlington, is scheduled to open fall 1996. TCJC's total unduplicated credit enrollment during fall 1994 was 26,253, making it the seventh largest college or university in Texas.

Distance learning at TCJC began in the early l970s when three courses were offered by instructional television (ITV). Steady growth, both in course offerings and enrollments, has since resulted, and ITV offerings now include 30 different courses.

Computer-delivered instruction (CDI) courses began in the spring of 1989 with one computer science course. CDI courses require students to access a computerized bulletin board system for delivery of instructional materials. Students download homework and assignments from the instructor, and upload homework and questions to the instructor. The proliferation of computers in homes has provided many students with the equipment necessary to enroll in a CDI course. Student and faculty interest in CDI has grown, and 11 courses have been developed; nine courses were offered in fall 1995 with enrollments totaling 261.

Interactive television courses involve a faculty member teaching a course live from a television studio at South Campus. Interactive classrooms located throughout the district receive the broadcast signal and display it on television monitors. Two-way communication is available between faculty members and students in the remote classrooms. Use of this technology facilitates the offering of specialized courses to small numbers of students at different locations.

CD-ROM instruction is a South Campus program that uses a stand-alone interactive textbook. This program, begun in 1993 with a course in United States History, presently offers two history courses each semester with enrollments totaling approximately 80 students.

The distance learning program includes all credit courses offered at locations other than one of the main campuses. One major component is the more than 30 college-credit course sections offered each semester at a high school in Arlington, Texas. Courses are offered evenings and Saturdays, and enrollments total approximately 1,000 students per semester. TCJC also works with other high schools to allow classes to be taken for both high school and college credit. In addition,

TCJC works with local businesses such as Tandy Corporation to provide college courses at their locations.

Program Overview

Students Served and Programs Offered

Distance learning enrollments totaled 11,653 from summer 1994 through spring 1995 and almost 200,000 students have been served by this approach since its inception at TCJC.

There is not a typical distance learning student, as virtually all students of the college are represented in the distance learning programs. This includes full- and part-time students right out of high school to more mature students returning to school or working on a degree a few courses at a time. The lifestyle of the average college student has changed dramatically during the past several years. Overall, students have more commitments, such as those involving jobs and/or families, and free time is limited. Some students, due to transportation problems or disabilities, prefer to limit their trips to campus and to do more of their learning at home.

Many students take one or two distance learning courses to supplement their on-campus schedules. University students often take distance learning courses at TCJC because of the convenience and cost effectiveness of the courses. Many students have requested that the number of courses offered through distance learning be increased. Sufficient demand exists to develop an associate's degree program that could be earned solely through distance learning.

ITV offerings include courses in science, business, English, government, history, health, music, philosophy, religion, psychology, and sociology. CDI offerings include courses in management, computer science, economics, English, and mathematics. CD-ROM offerings include two history courses. Many textbooks are now available via interactive CD, and faculty in several disciplines are exploring this technology with an eye to using it in classrooms or as stand-alone course offerings. Interactive television course offerings have included courses in engineering, mathematics, computer science, and nutrition. Off-campus offerings have primarily been university-parallel courses, although numerous other courses have been offered periodically.

Administrators and faculty involved in distance learning overwhelmingly feel that distance learning courses complement on-campus offerings and do not affect enrollments in on-campus offerings of the same courses. The quality of the courses is the same—only the instructional mode is different.

Program Organization

The program is organized and operated through the Educational Affairs staff of the college.

The director of Distance Learning, a district employee with an office on the South Campus, oversees the distance learning programs for all district campuses. The director reports to the vice chancellor for educational affairs, who coordinates all educational programs in the district and reports directly to the chancellor. An administrative office assistant provides support services to the director. The assistant director of distance learning is responsible for the day-to-day operations of the Center for Distance Learning, and works with the director to develop distance learning policies, procedures, and programs.

The assistant director supervises a support staff of four full-time employees and seven half-time employees. The Center for Distance Learning operates a centralized hotline and message center and prepares and distributes instructional course materials. Center personnel provide assistance to faculty and students, ensuring that details necessary for the smooth operation of all distance learning programs are addressed.

Faculty input, along with the involvement of the academic department and division chairpersons, is always an integral part of any distance learning course from development to the actual offering. Committees composed of faculty and administrators from all campuses meet to determine the academic credibility of and the logistics of offering any course. Faculty are assigned to the distance learning program through their on-campus departments and divisions and officially report to these individuals, but they are also responsible to, work closely with, and communicate extensively with distance learning administrators. Faculty from all three college campuses have been and are currently involved in distance learning. In most cases, a faculty member instructs all students in the district who are enrolled in a particular course. The faculty member is available on all campuses periodically throughout the semester at orientation and seminars. Faculty normally receive one course (three-hour load) credit for teaching the course; in the case of higher enrollment courses, the load credit assigned is sometimes higher. In the courses where instructor contact is more intense, such as science and English courses, a faculty member may be assigned on each campus.

Distance learning programs are funded by the college through a yearly operating budget. This budget funds all operating expenses such as printing costs, broadcast fees, per student lease fees, and provides for supplies and equipment. Students are not assessed additional fees for enrolling in a course through distance learning. ITV students can lease telelesson videos for a $10 nonrefundable fee which is deposited in the distance learning account to cover the cost of producing and maintaining the lease kits.

Instructional Strategies

Distance learning programs follow the typical semester pattern used by the college, i.e., 16-week semesters for fall and spring, and two six-week summer sessions.

Registration is held concurrently with registration for on-campus courses, and students must attend a mandatory orientation session for all distance learning courses during the first week of the semester.

Instructional strategies vary between the programs. A committee composed of faculty members and appropriate administrators reviews proposals for any distance learning course. Once approval has been given, the instructional methods and strategies are developed. For ITV courses, the primary method of instruction is the telelesson series; for CD-ROM instruction, the interactive textbook serves as the primary instructional tool. CDI, interactive, and off-campus instructors develop all instructional materials used in addition to their textbooks. CDI instructors provide students with files on a computerized bulletin board system that include chapter and lecture notes, homework, and assignments. Interactive and off-campus faculty develop their classroom materials in the same manner as any faculty member teaching in the classroom would. All distance learning faculty are responsible for the development of any additional instructional materials used, such as those used for orientations and seminars, test reviews, and exams.

Technologies Employed

ITV courses are broadcast over PBS (KDTN) and/or cable television. In addition, viewing centers with televisions and VCRs are available in each campus library for use when students are on campus. TCJC broadcasts courses over KDTN with other colleges in the Dallas-Fort Worth metroplex, such as Dallas County Community College, and shares the broadcast fees for using this service. TCJC also broadcasts almost all ITV courses over four cable companies in Tarrant County through the Instructional Television Fixed Services (ITFS) department of the college. ITFS is responsible for broadcasting courses on cable television, working in conjunction with the assistant director of distance learning to produce the semester and weekly cable logs. This technology is managed by a television systems engineer, an assistant television systems engineer, and a support person who oversees air-switching the programs. TCJC has an agreement with the cable companies to have the installation fee waived for students enrolled in an ITV course.

TCJC broadcasts its signal from the South Campus to a receiver site in downtown Fort Worth. The signal is then sent to the cable companies. TCJC has four channels and uses one for ITV, one for interactive television, and the remaining two for broadcasting teleconferences. Interactive television originates in a broadcast studio in which the instructor works two video cameras, one positioned to face the instructor and the other ceiling mounted to view any writing the instructor would like to appear on the screen. A two-way telephone system allows for interaction between the students and the instructor. Television monitors are located in each classroom for students to view the instructor live. ITFS staff train the instructors in the use of the broadcast studio.

The computerized bulletin board system for CDI is operated by a system operator on the Distance Learning staff. The software used is PCBoard. Four telephone lines are dedicated for student use, and two lines are reserved for faculty.

The system operator is responsible for training faculty in the use of the bulletin board system and conducts orientations and enrichment seminars for students in the use of the board. The advantage to students using this mode of learning is that they can access the bulletin board from anywhere at any time. Students who travel as part of their jobs report that this convenience often means the difference in being able to enroll in a college-credit course or not.

Students are able to purchase the CD interactive textbooks for use at home in Macintosh or Windows formats. Access to computer labs and learning centers on South Campus assures that students have access to the hardware and software necessary to succeed in these courses. Support staff are available in the labs and at orientations to demonstrate the CD and answer questions.

Student Services Provided

All TCJC students, including distance learning students, follow regular application and admittance procedures. Students are given a schedule of orientation dates and times when they register for a distance learning course. This information also includes information regarding textbooks, study guides, and materials that are available at all TCJC bookstores, as well as at several off-campus, privately run bookstores.

Student services are provided on each campus, and students may participate in any student service activity on the campus of their choice. In any distance learning course, students may attend orientations and seminars and take their exams on any campus.

Students meet their instructors at orientations and again periodically throughout the semester at seminars. Instructors have scheduled office hours and can be contacted via phone or mail

Counseling facilities are available for academic advising on each campus, and distance learning students are encouraged to take advantage of this service. All campus laboratories, such as the Writing Center, Computer Science labs, and the Computer Learning Center are available to distance learning students.

Students may obtain assistance on procedural or administrative issues from the Center for Distance Learning, a district operating center housed on South Campus. A centralized phone message center allows students to call with questions regarding testing times and locations, withdrawal procedures, or other procedural questions. Students may also meet with the center staff in person on South Campus to discuss these issues.

Student Grading and Program Evaluation

Student progress is measured primarily on the basis of exams. Exams may be objective, essay, or a combination and are administered by distance learning and testing center staff on each campus. Some courses require that papers or other assignments also be completed, and some base a portion of the grade on participation, either at seminars (in the case of ITV), or on the bulletin board system (some CDI courses).

All ITV and CD-ROM records are kept on a computerized records management program. Teachers are given a computerized printout of their gradebook after each graded activity. The records manager, a member of the distance learning staff, is responsible for organizing, verifying, and maintaining all paperwork relating to ITV and CD-ROM students. Due to the smaller size classes in CDI, interactive television, and off-campus courses, faculty teaching through these modes of instruction maintain their own gradebooks.

Student evaluations are administered yearly in ITV and CD-ROM classes. CDI instructors are evaluated each semester due to the ease of evaluation administration using the bulletin board system. Instructors for off-campus and interactive television courses are evaluated by on-campus administrators on a periodic basis. Input from all student evaluations is sent to the instructor and appropriate administrators. Instructors often incorporate the suggestions and comments received in future course offerings.

Unique or Exemplary Practices

The Center for Distance Learning began offering instructional television courses in January 1995 to inmates at the Federal Medical Center–Fort Worth (FMC), and the Federal Medical Center–Carswell. These students shared some unique educational needs, and distance learning provided the flexibility they required for completing coursework.

Distance learning administrators knew that, logistically, ITV courses could easily be offered to the students. Since FMC is conveniently located near the South Campus, an initial planning meeting included appropriate personnel from FMC, distance learning administrators, and the South Campus registrar and bursar, who discussed the concerns and logistics of registering these students and receiving their fees and tuition. This initial meeting confirmed the belief that this educational endeavor would be possible.

An educational staff member from FMC was designated to serve as the liaison between the prison and TCJC personnel in matters concerning the students. The FMC coordinator worked with the South Campus registrar and bursar to provide the necessary paperwork for the students to be admitted to the college and was responsible for registering these students, making sure their tuition and fees were paid, and that books and materials were purchased.

Once the students were officially registered in the course, the FMC coordinator worked with distance learning administrators on strategies that would enable FMC students to fulfill course requirements. All distance learning students are required to attend an orientation session for each course in which they are enrolled. To enable FMC students to complete the orientation requirement, faculty members audiotaped an orientation session. Orientation materials such as course booklets and paperwork were given to the FMC coordinator, who in turn made sure the students completed the orientation requirements by listening to the audiotape, reading the course booklet, and completing the required paperwork. Authorization forms granting permission for the FMC coordinator to discuss students' grades and coursework with the instructor and/or distance learning administrators, were also completed by the student. All paperwork was then returned to the Center for Distance Learning.

A set of telelessons was provided to FMC; their educational offices are equipped with a television and VCR, enabling students to view their lessons. Students purchased their own copies of textbooks and study guides and were able to study at their convenience. Supplemental materials, such as test reviews, handouts, and audiotapes of seminars and review sessions were mailed to the FMC coordinator to be distributed to the appropriate students.

The FMC coordinator picked up all exam materials from the Center for Distance Learning and arranged dates and times for each student to take exams. Exams were administered at the prison in a secure environment and were proctored by the FMC coordinator. The completed exams were returned to the Center for Distance Learning for grading. Grade receipts were then given to the FMC coordinator to distribute to the students.

Twelve faculty members have been involved in offering courses to FMC, and students have been enrolled in 14 different courses since the program began in January of 1995. Enrollments have been small, but the program is growing and has already been deemed successful. In spite of their confined status, prisoners were able to be college students and earn college credit, thereby increasing their chances of success on release.

Kevin R. Eason
Tarrant County Junior College District
South Campus
828 Harwood Road
Hurst, TX 76054
(817) 531-6016; fax: (817) 531-6086

Carolyn C. Robertson
Tarrant County Junior College District
South Campus
828 Harwood Road
Hurst, TX 76054
(817) 531-4532; fax: (817) 531-6086

Chapter 15

UNIVERSITY COLLEGE OF THE CARIBOO'S LEARNING NETWORK
Kamloops, British Columbia

Adrian Kershaw

The University College of the Cariboo's Learning Network was established to serve the needs of small population centres scattered over an area of 60,000 square miles in south central British Columbia, Canada. Increasing rates of economic and social change in the 1980s created a growing demand for postsecondary education from the region's population of 200,000. The residents of the small communities the college serves were facing the realities of increasing obsolescence of workplace skills and growing structural unemployment. But many students were place-bound, unable through force of geography or personal situation to access training and education at the college's main campus in Kamloops or at the many postsecondary institutions in the Vancouver/Victoria area. By the early 1990s, it had become clear that UCC could not respond to the breadth of demand through the use of traditional fixed classroom delivery methods. Accordingly, a decision was made to expand the institution's relatively modest distance-delivery function and to employ advanced communications technologies to augment and extend training and education services wherever possible.

In the spring of 1993, UCC undertook a major review of its distance delivery function. This review pointed the way to the need to rationalize some of the distance education offerings, to develop new courses, and to contemplate the use of the new digital communications technologies which were just becoming practicable in British Columbia. Faculty, administrators, and college board members visited a number of institutions in the United States and attended two key conferences (at the University of Maine and the League for Innovation's conference in Tennessee) in the fall of 1993.

An action plan was developed which drew on the best practices of other institutions. This plan was presented to the provincial government and approved for special funding in the summer of 1994. Fortuitously, at the same time as UCC was developing its educational telecommunications plan, BC Telecom—one of the local telephone companies—had been laying fiber-optic cable up the main north-south axis of the college region and had begun to install asynchronous transfer mode switches at its major nodes in the southern part of the province. This development enabled UCC to use full-motion interactive video transmission in conjunction with other educational telecommunications technologies in the creation of its Learning Network.

From the early stages of planning for this new initiative three central themes were emphasized:

- that distance education as a means of improving access to rural populations is a responsibility of all faculty and staff;
- that the focus is on teaching and learning rather than on the technology;
- that the role of the instructional staff is key to the success of the initiative.

UCC is now actively involved in the development of a distributed learning environment which links postsecondary institutions and schools across the province.

Program Overview

As a regional college, UCC has always been faced with the challenge of reaching out from its full-service campus in Kamloops to the rest of its catchment area. The response has been to establish a campus at Williams Lake which provides a limited range of vocational, career/technical, first and second-year university courses, and continuing education opportunities to a population of about 11,000 people. A third level of infrastructure has come into being since the late 1980s with the establishment of five small training and education centres in communities with populations between 2,000 and 6,000. These third-order campuses provide continuing education, employment-related training, and some academic programming on an as-needed basis. The remaining five small villages (populations below 2,000) are supported principally through employment-related continuing education offerings.

All of the regional operations are characterized, however, by demand for a wide range of courses from a relatively small number of students. Only occasionally has it been possible to put together sufficient numbers of students to expand service in a cost-effective fashion. And, even if sufficient demand exists, finding appropriately qualified staff locally has been impossible in many cases. It was in this context that the emergence of educational telecommunications presented the college with a cost-effective means of meeting these needs across its region.

Instructional Strategies

The administrative structure of the Learning Network reflects UCC's desire to have its faculty and administrative staff view distance delivery as a viable means of meeting the needs of the remote communities served. Rather than have a centralized distance delivery office responsible for the function, UCC has chosen to distribute responsibility for the courses and their delivery into the various academic departments. In addition, administrative and technical support are provided by existing structures and procedures. By these means, UCC has been able to escape a common pitfall of centralized distance delivery systems, namely, that the function is seen as being "somebody else's problem." To counter this tendency, UCC has taken steps to ensure that all instructional divisions have a role to play in using the new technologies for delivery and that the technical staff are seen as supporters rather than leaders of the project.

Before instructional staff were recruited to use the new technologies, however, a contractual agreement was reached with the faculty union on the use of the new delivery methods. This agreement included recompense for the additional effort needed to prepare materials to use with educational telecommunications and a guarantee that the technology would not be used to displace existing instructors in smaller centres. Also, the two parties to the agreement recognized that the emerging Learning Network was *terra incognita* and, therefore, agreed to form a joint monitoring team to review progress and to make recommendations for later contract language in the light of experience. The college saw this agreement as a pivotal element in the likely success of the Learning Network and held back on plan implementation until the agreement was in place.

Following the signing of the contractual agreement, instructors were deliberately recruited from each of the five instructional divisions to be among the first to use ITV and computer conferencing. In addition, to make the point that the technology was not "owned" by instructional staff at the main campus in Kamloops, the facilities in Williams Lake and Merritt were identically equipped with ITV and other advanced communications technologies. Thus, the delivery of service from any of the three principle campuses of UCC is practicable.

In early investigations of practice in other distance education programs it was recognized that frequently student learning in distance delivery settings has been "shoehorned" into the available technology, often to the detriment of the learning process. Instructors at UCC are encouraged to "map" the various instructional technologies (print, e-mail, computer conferencing, teleconferencing, World Wide Web, interactive video, videotape, audiotape, and face-to-face) against the curriculum elements.

As a consequence, hybrid delivery systems are being generated which are often unique to individual instructors and courses. The relationship between instructor and student is beginning to change. Students are becoming actively involved in their own learning as instructors develop materials and teaching methods which cast them in the role of learning facilitator.

Students are provided with an orientation to the technology found in the ITV environment. Each student receives a student guide, which is structured in a question and answer format. This guide gives students an idea of what they can expect in an ITV course and what is expected of them.

Considerable resources have been allocated to professional development and technical and administrative support. Orientation and training workshops are held, departments are encouraged to use ITV for their meetings, experienced faculty act as mentors, and training manuals have been developed. In addition, instructors have access to secretarial assistance for the development of student manuals and for the transcription of text. A graphics technician is available to instructors who need to generate graphics for use in manuals, ITV, and the World Wide Web. Finally, site coordinators at each of the smaller centers are assigned to assist instructors with such things as collecting and handing out assignments, supervision of examinations, and basic technical trouble shooting.

Academic control of the courses resides with the department of record, whatever the source of funding. This matrix organizational model was adopted as part of the overall strategy to embed responsibility for distributed learning systems in the instructional divisions rather than to establish a separate function. Telecommunications costs for all the activity are currently absorbed into a special budget set aside to support the project.

Student Services Provided

UCC's system of five community coordinators located in the smaller centres, five training and education centres in the region's medium-sized centres, and staff at its two main campuses in Williams Lake and Kamloops provides a range of support systems for students using the Learning Network. Students taking courses through the two main campuses have face-to-face access to a full range of student support services such as admissions and records, libraries, bookstores, and counseling and advising. For courses offered at the three remote ITV sites—Williams Lake, 100 Mile House, and Merritt—site coordinators provide logistical support to the instructional process. Learning Network students can access the library catalogue by modem and order materials by e-mail or phone. These materials are then mailed or couriered to the nearest UCC site. UCC personnel handle admissions and registration documents, sell texts and other course materials to place-bound students, and assist students resolve administrative problems. Each of the centres outside of Kamloops and Williams Lake provides access to college and university calendars and telephone access to advising and counseling services. Where appropriate, UCC personnel also organize group study activities to help reduce the isolation of some place-bound students.

Students Served and Programs Offered

The courses identified for delivery over the Learning Network are drawn from all instructional divisions. Initial offerings using the new technologies were lecture/seminar courses from first- and second-year degree programs. More recently, university and upgrading courses with laboratory and practicum elements have been offered. These courses have used a combination of appropriate educational telecommunications methods and face-to-face laboratory or practical experiences. In addition, employment-related training in the fields of mental health and transportation have been offered using ITV. Planning is also underway to use educational telecommunications in conjunction with on-the-job training in two apprenticeship programs. A variety of professional development opportunities for high school teachers and American Sign Language instructors will be offered in 1996.

In terms of overall service, UCC is using the Learning Network in two ways. First, the new technologies are being used to provide interactive access to postsecondary credit courses for the first time in many of the smaller communities in the service area. The second kind of service is one of augmentation. The Learning Network has enabled UCC to deliver courses—especially upper-level university courses in areas such as nursing—to its second largest campus in Williams Lake that otherwise would not be available to students at that campus. These courses are often low-enrollment courses, yet students in Williams Lake must have access to them to complete their degrees.

The Learning Network has allowed the University College to meet these needs in a cost and educationally effective manner. In addition, programming in Williams Lake is augmented with courses delivered by the University of Northern British Columbia, which uses UCC's educational telecommunications and regular classroom facilities.

Technologies Employed

The technology infrastructure plan was divided into three phases:

- Phase 1 encompassed the establishment of the instructional support facilities and the installation of ITV suites in Kamloops, Williams Lake, and Merritt. The fiber-optic link between Kamloops and Williams Lake provides full-motion video, while the Merritt link uses 384 kbps compressed video. At the same time, e-mail and Internet capabilities were upgraded and a Multiple Academic User Domain (MAUD) installed to support virtual classroom capabilities. Six school districts and UCC signed an agreement in principle to form an educational telecommunications consortium to exploit the potential for improved access to secondary and postsecondary services and to reduce the potential for facility duplication.
- Phase 2 saw the installation of an ITV suite in 100 Mile House (owned by UCC) and the installation of ITV suites by School District 24 (Kamloops) in Chase and Barriere, and in Clearwater by the North Thompson Community Skills Center. The link to 100 Mile House is over fiber-optic cable while the school district links use 112 kbps service. E-mail service and Internet connections have been provided by UCC and the school districts involved to these locations.
- Phase 3 will see the expansion of ITV service to the training and education centres at Lillooet and Ashcoft/Cache Creek. Internet connections will be provided in these locations in cooperation with the local school districts.

The last phase will ensure that the vast majority of potential students in the college region are all within one hour's drive or less of a UCC site where there is access to ITV and other educational telecommunications.

The infrastructure plan also foresees the emergence of linkages with institutions and schools both inside and outside of the college region. UCC came to the conclusion that it must cooperate to improve access to programs and courses delivered by and to other agencies. It was this realization which led the institution to propose the formation of the telecommunications consortium with its school district partners, the first step in the development of a distributed learning environment.

The realization of the institution's educational telecommunications plan has been greatly helped by the partnership between UCC and BC Telecom. The telephone company has provided technical assistance, initial technical and instructor training, and line rate subsidy. In addition, the vendors of the ITV equipment have proven to be very supportive in helping the institution and its partners resolve technical challenges. This kind of after-sales service has been of great importance to UCC since it was determined from the start of the project that the technology should interfere as little as possible with the teaching function. Technological transparency is particularly important as UCC cannot afford to have a technician present to manipulate the equipment. The instructors are solely responsible for the classroom operation and, hence, need a technical infrastructure which is simple to operate, reliable, and of as high a quality as possible.

Unique or Exemplary Practices

UCC decided that the organizing theme for its use of educational telecommunications would be to "focus on the people not the technology." It was also determined that in order to limit the marginalization of distance delivery common in other organizations it was important to embed responsibility for the Learning Network in the academic divisions of the institution. Furthermore, it was felt that the institution had to show that it had a strong commitment to professional development in the area of educational telecommunications.

As a result, UCC has implemented a comprehensive series of training opportunities that have had a great impact on the college's efforts in distance learning. The two-day training events are structured around material drawn from an Instructional Skills Workshop (ISW) which was developed for use throughout the province by a consortium of colleges. Most instructors have taken the ISW and are comfortable with the concepts, practices, and terminology used. The trainers then apply those understandings to teaching in a distributed learning environment. As a consequence, participants have a high comfort level because they are learning about the new techniques on a foundation of familiar practice.

Instructors are provided with time to play with the various technologies under the guidance of the training staff. This "mucking about" period is a critical element in the demystification of the technology, a process which is essential if instructors are to be able to operate effectively without a technician in the classroom at all times. During this experimental period, instructors begin to explore their personal comfort levels with the technology. Some may be satisfied to use a "talking head" approach to delivery to begin with, but eventually start to use the technology in ways which enhance student learning.

On the second day of the training event, the participants present a 10- to 15-minute mini-lesson prepared during the previous evening. They are encouraged to use as much or as little of the technology as their comfort level allows. At the end of each presentation, the rest of the trainers and the other trainees provide feedback on the presenter's teaching and use of the technologies. Instructors can make videotapes of their presentations for later review if they wish.

Once instructors are using ITV to deliver courses, additional training is provided. Several instructors have taken training on the integration of the computer conferencing into the teaching/learning process. In particular, the instructors have been trained on the use of UCC's MAUD facility to provide virtual classroom, office, and seminar room experience for students. Also, many instructors have been trained on the use of presentation software to generate graphics for use on the microcomputers linked to the ITV

classroom. Finally, once World Wide Web access is available at the college's ITV sites, training will be provided to instructors on how to integrate that technology into their course delivery systems.

While not strictly part of the training program, the use of ITV for departmental and other meetings is a highly effective means of introducing a wide range of instructors and staff to the new technology. Thus, when instructors eventually come for training on the use of ITV, they already have some idea of what they are going to see when they walk in to the ITV classrooms.

Adrian Kershaw
Dean, Developmental and Regional Programs
The University College of the Cariboo
900 McGill Road, Box 3010
Kamloops, B.C. V2C 5N3
(604) 828-5163; fax: (604) 371-5514
e-mail: akershaw@cariboo.bc.ca

Chapter 16

WASHTENAW COMMUNITY COLLEGE
Ann Arbor, Michigan

Edith Jacques and Richard Cooper

Washtenaw Community College (WCC) was created by the voters of Washtenaw County, Michigan, in 1964, when an increase in the county's industrial research and development activities resulted in a growing demand for more highly trained personnel and skilled technicians.

Today the college exists as a comprehensive community college with an enrollment of just over 10,000 students. WCC employs 170 full-time faculty and 450 part-time faculty throughout the academic year. Credit programs of study cover 73 areas in business, health, math, natural sciences, public services, humanities, and the social sciences.

WCC's service area includes parts of three counties located in Southeastern Michigan: Washtenaw, Wayne (City of Belleville and Van Buren Township), and Livingston (the Brighton, Pickney, and Hartland areas) and is defined as the geographical areas from which the college draws the greatest number of students. This area encompasses approximately 858 square miles.

Program Overview

Throughout its history, WCC has been committed to making quality academic programs available to as many citizens in its service area as can benefit from them. The college sees this commitment as pertaining especially to its two primary student populations, the adult worker and (in consistently increasing numbers) the newly graduated high school student.

In determining which delivery systems would provide the access needed by students, Washtenaw Community College has always used the following criteria to guide its actions: First, the college mission and student needs must be the primary factors in determining what delivery systems, including distance learning, to provide for its students. Second, the value of and justification for a distance education program, like other programs regardless of delivery system, is determined by how well it can respond to the service area's need for multiaccess instructional models.

During WCC's early years, this philosophy led to the development of what could be considered "a multiple options" approach to the delivery of instruction. From the late 1960s until spring 1975, the college followed what was really a decentralized model to administer all its delivery systems. Through both its organizational structure (a main campus, four regional centers, and 21 different extension sites), and by making available a variety of delivery modes and instructional formats, the college attempted to respond to the access needs of its students. These delivery and format options included classes at various extension sites such as shopping centers, malls and churches; dedicated classrooms at manufacturing plants; independent study; instructor-coordinated, self-paced, math labs; cooperative experiences; and apprenticeship training.

Program Organization

With the development of the Continuing Education office in 1975, a coordinated decentralized approach was used to administer the program. The director of that office coordinated daily operations of delivery options programs which were, at that point, primarily extension programs.

Although these delivery options did provide increased accessibility for place-bound students (and served 137,702 students between 1981 and 1995), they did not address numerous other obstacles which rendered college courses, programs, and services inaccessible to some students.

By winter semester 1982, the college increased accessibility by initiating its first real option in distance education, a telecourse program. At the same time, WCC assumed a leadership role in the development of two consortia, the Educational Teleconsortium of Michigan, the first statewide consortium of this type, and the Southeastern Michigan Educational Television Consortium. Washtenaw was a charter member in both consortia and, as such, helped establish guidelines for licensing fees, "group buys" for preproduced courses, airing fees, airing times, and student fees.

Technologies Employed

The telecourse program consists of prerecorded telecourses offered over the service area's public access and cable network channels. This approach employs one-way video, supported by a telephone hotline.

Instructional Strategies

An on-campus, single-session orientation is held with the instructor. The phone is used, along with the U.S. mail, for additional communication and transporting of materials. In 1992, the program established a tape check-out service at the Learning Resource Center where copies of the telecourse tapes are available for telecourse students to check out for a week at a time.

Faculty can request to teach a telecourse or extension course, or the department chair (in consultation with the dean) can schedule such an arrangement as part of an instructor's semester schedule. The departmental instructional budgets supports faculty salaries, which are determined by the faculty union contract. Contract language established load credit of three contact hours for student enrollments between 15 and 70 students. Any number above 70 qualifies faculty for pay and load rates associated with large lectures. Approximately 98 percent of telecourse instruction is provided by full-time faculty. There is no difference in pay for teaching an extension class from one scheduled on campus.

The daily supervision and coordination of the Telecourse Program is the responsibility of the dean of the Continuing Education Division, in consultation with the appropriate divisional dean and department chair.

Student Grading and Evaluation

The college has always ensured that telecourses and extension courses are equivalent in content to any other section of that course that is delivered via traditional means, whether taught on campus or off. Therefore grades and grading standards are determined as for any other class. Distance learning and extension instructors must comply with all college, departmental, and divisional policies.

Student Services Provided

Although admissions, registration, and counseling services were made available on a limited basis at the regional centers by the early 1980s, none were available via distance delivery technology for telecourse or extension students. At the time, the college lacked the technology to support providing academic services via distance delivery systems, and staff did not have the needed training to deliver services in this way. By 1993, modems were installed at the regional centers for registration purposes, but exams still had to be taken on campus in a testing center.

Even with these limitations, the Telecourse Program did offer some solutions to time and location barriers which the Extension Program did not, and served 7,645 students between winter 1982 and fall 1995. From 1988 to the present, the program has offered an average of 10 courses during fall and winter semesters and six during spring and summer.

During this period, the college continued to work strategically with its existing community partnerships for the purpose of resource sharing. Partnerships were viewed as a means to better enable WCC to provide for its students through distance learning delivery and build potential for resource sharing to support future delivery options as they appeared. An important example of this use of "technology partnerships" is the college's membership in the Technology Learning Exchange, which includes the Washtenaw County Intermediate School District, the 10 local school districts in Washtenaw County, Eastern Michigan University, the University of Michigan, and the Washtenaw County Library System. The Exchange is a consortium whose purposes are to ensure the compatibility of equipment over a countywide cable network that provides cable connections to all schools, colleges and homes in the county; to increase opportunities to access existing equipment; and to provide training and other resources to members.

Unique or Exemplary Practices

WCC's distance learning delivery options remained limited to telecourses until mid-1992. At this point, the college began to identify courses that could be taken via distance

learning to fulfill certain curriculum requirements in the evening and weekend degree program for accounting and business management.

In 1993, WCC became an active player in CoNDUIT (Cooperative Network for Dual-Use Technology Information), an international project intended to link together a network of community colleges with manufacturing expertise and develop innovative mechanisms for disseminating manufacturing education to small and medium size businesses.

CoNDUIT enabled the college, for the first time, to see the impact of a changing environment on its approach to instructional design (and delivery systems) and the need to change this approach. CoNDUIT formed the technical foundation for advancement of a completely new instructional design concept that resulted in a new distance learning plan for WCC.

It very quickly became apparent that the college had to redefine its concept of instructional design to reflect new parameters, to serve as a guide for the development of all the college's curriculum and delivery modes, and to outline future directions for needed technology applications. To accomplish this, WCC established a Commission on Instructional Design, a Co-Convenor's Group, and a Networking Action Team.

The work of the Co-Convenor's Group (working in coordination with the Network Action Team and the Commission) resulted in a resolve to ensure the availability and appropriate use of technology to support the instructional development and delivery plan, regardless of the delivery mode. This plan is intended to carry the college far beyond the more fundamental "multiple options" approach which, through the extension centers concept, had provided additional options for location-bound students, and with the Telecourse Program, some solutions to time barriers.

The Commission also developed a definition of distance learning and instructional design and used these as the basis for developing the distance learning plan and model. Instructional design is understood to be "a process in which every aspect of delivering instruction to students (including delivery methods, time and place factors, staffing, and student outcomes) is examined, organized, and evaluated with the purposes of continually enhancing learning." Distance learning is defined as "the process of extending learning or delivering instructional resource sharing opportunities to locations away from a classroom, building, or site (including work sites and individual homes), by using video, audio, computer, multimedia communications, or some combination of these with other traditional delivery methods."

The strategic goal of WCC's Distance Learning Program, as it now exists, is to support the college in its efforts to become more accessible and to provide quality instruction for students. A key strategy is to form technology partnerships with other educational institutions, businesses, and industries, and human service and government entities to increase access to needed services, materiel, and human resources. The very foundation of WCC's distance learning model, as well as many of the individual programs and services which fall within it, relies on such collaboration.

The college is using the collective accomplishments and

resources of its partnerships to gain and/or increase WCC's presence in its service area in multiple ways. Libraries and schools serve as video-receive sites, while other sites, including businesses, receive instruction via the Internet or satellite. The partnership between WCC, the school district, and EMU decreases replication of costs and supports shared access to a variety of data. This access provides opportunities for students to find information on articulation, placement, counseling, career planning services—and even develop electronic educational development plans. Among the other benefits that have accrued to WCC's students as a result of partnership activities are:

- Complete courses developed and instructed over the Internet using the World Wide Web and other Internet technology, such as a course in "How to Teach Simulation"; computer numeric control courses (as well as networked-based information applications); and a Robotics Technology associate's degree taught over the Internet and employing simulation techniques in the instruction. These courses and techniques are being developed for replication and use as models for other community colleges.
- The college uses a variety of different distant delivery modes (the Internet, compressed video/interactive classroom, and e-mail) to offer student services, tutoring, shared professional development for partners, dual enrollment opportunities for high school and EMU students, customized training for business and industry, credentialing and updating for professions, and teleconferencing to provide certification.
- A collaborative, program-driven development center offers opportunities for shared professional development among WCC, EMU, and school district faculty/staff in curriculum development and instruction of distance learning via traditional and distance learning technologies. For example, WCC has hosted a series of teleconferences such as *Violence in the Classroom*, and *Using Computers to Teach and Learn*, as part of the shared professional development program for EMU, WCC, and school district faculties.
- WCC's CyberSpace Station provides support for the design and authoring of high-level interactive training programs, repurposing of videodiscs, authoring and mastering of CD-ROMs, and computer-managed instruction and testing.

- The CoNDUIT Small Business Center Project uses the Internet to provide information and training to small businesses. The Small Business Development Center and WCC's Workplace Learning Program also use the Internet to place cooperative education students into workplace experiences.
- The Learning Technologies Exchange makes effective, continuous education accessible to a broad array of students and community populations.
- Multiple college extension centers are located conveniently around WCC's service area, with access to interactive networks linking them to each other and the main campus via portable and/or permanent interactive (compressed video) electronic classrooms and Internet hook-ups.

WCC has just begun to realize the possibilities and benefits that the distance learning program can provide for students and the community at large. All the elements critical to success are now in place: the partnerships, critical for community and financial support; the student-centered instruction, curricula, and delivery systems which are needed to provide quality, relevant, and accessible curricula; and updated technology and continuous development and training for all involved. WCC's evolving distance learning program is well positioned to meet the needs of students for many years to come.

Edith Jacques
Dean of Alternative Education
Washtenaw Community College
P. O. Box D-1
4800 East Huron River Drive
Ann Arbor, Michigan 48106
(313) 677-5003; fax: (313) 677-5045
e-mail: ejacques@orchard.washtenaw.cc.mi.us

Richard Cooper
Director, Learning Technologies Department
Washtenaw Community College
P. O. Box D-1
4800 East Huron River Drive
Ann Arbor, Michigan 48106
(313) 677-3302; fax: (313) 677-5045
e-mail: rcooper@orchard.washtenaw.cc.mi.us

Appendix
ANNOTATED LISTING OF DISTANCE EDUCATION PROGRAMS

In the spring of 1996, as detailed in the introduction, colleges across North America were invited to submit descriptions of their distance learning programs to a national panel charged with identifying exemplary or model distance learning efforts in community colleges. The panel, which included recognized leaders in distance education from across the continent, faced a difficult task as it set about deciding which of the many colleges that submitted program abstracts would be featured in a planned publication devoted to the state-of-the-art in distance education.

The panel felt strongly that many of the colleges that submitted abstracts in the original call for proposals were extraordinary in some way. Unfortunately, space limitations prohibited the inclusion of all these worthy colleges in featured chapters, but the panel felt some recognition of the contributions of these colleges should be attempted. This annotated listing of outstanding distance learning programs is intended to address that recommendation by providing readers with a thumbnail sketch of each program. Colleges are listed alphabetically and contact persons have been included so that additional detail may be obtained if desired.

Bismarck State College, Bismarck, North Dakota

Bismarck State College (BSC) is active in two major distance learning efforts. The Interactive Video Network (IVN) connects North Dakota's 11 institutions of higher education; Great Western Network (GWN) is a consortium of 19 rural public schools in Central North Dakota. IVN has been used to bring graduate and baccalaureate programs to the BSC campus. Through the GWN, Bismarck State College sends its courses to high school seniors and adults who would otherwise have to drive from 40 to 80 miles to campus. The BSC interactive video experience is unique in that the college is a receiver of education over IVN and a sender over GWN.

Contact: Pat Gross, IVN/ITV Coordinator; Bismarck State College, 1500 Edwards Avenue, Bismarck, ND 58501; (701) 224-5484, fax: (701) 224-5552.

Bossier Parish Community College, Bossier City, Louisiana

Bossier Parish Community College operates its own Public Education and Government (PEG) cable channel which reaches almost every school in the district. This 24-hour programming responsibility is operated by students and includes four live programs daily: "Newsbreak," "Coffeebreak," "Homework Hotline," and "Evening Update." A microwave transmission and receiving facility link a mobile production van to two studios housed at the South Campus facility.

Contact: Larry Powell, Director of Telecommunications; Bossier Parish Community College, 2900 Douglas Drive, Bossier City, LA 71111; (318) 746-7754, fax: (318) 747-3364.

Brookdale Community College, Lincroft, New Jersey

Brookdale Community offers Monmouth County residents an opportunity to earn college credit by taking college courses via radio, television, and/or an individual-use tape option. Currently, credits earned are applied to an existing degree program offered by the various academic departments. Brookdale is in the process, however, of initiating a degree program in Liberal Studies which would allow a student to earn an A.A. degree taking only telecourse classes.

Generally, Brookdale offers 16 to 20 courses during each of the 15-week fall and winter semesters and three courses during the 12-week spring and summer terms. Brookdale uses its own 11,000-watt radio station to offer the radio telecourses and local cable systems, the state of New Jersey Cable Television Network, and the state's public television station (the New Jersey Network) as outlets for the television programs. Brookdale also participates in PBS' national "Going the Distance" project.

Contact: Louis Pullano, Division Director of Arts and Communication; Brookdale Community College, 765 Newman Springs Road, Lincroft, NJ 07738; (908) 224-2491, fax: (908) 747-7107.

Butte Community College, Oroville, California

Serving the counties of Butte and Glenn in Northern California, Butte Community College began its distance learning program in the early 1970s. Since then, it has evolved into a program offering 35 to 40 courses over television (ITFS) each semester with a student enrollment of 2,500 per year. The college programs four channels daily, five days a week during the fall, spring, and summer semesters. All credits earned by students apply to degree programs offered by the various instructional departments of the college.

Course offerings are both prerecorded and live/interactive. Prerecorded courses are transmitted to local cable companies for distribution to 10 towns and cities, consisting of over 55,000 homes. Students view programming on television and use the telephone and mail to contact instructors and return assignments. Approximately half of all prerecorded courses are produced by

Butte College instructors in the college's television studio.

Most recently, the college has implemented a return video system from its two remote centers to facilitate live/interactive courses. The return system allows the student's image and voice to appear in the main campus originating classroom. The instructor recognizes the student at the remote center as he does any student in the classroom. Students at remote centers are located in carrels, each equipped with a monitor and receiver, a miniature television camera to pick up the student's image, a headset with a small microphone to listen and to talk, and a push button that when pressed sends the student's compressed picture and voice over ISDN line back to the originating classroom. Since the system design requires only two personal computers with supporting software (one at the distant site and one in the originating classroom) to connect 20 or more individual carrels, costs are kept very low.

Contact: Robert Ellsworth, Media Coordinator; Butte Community College, 3536 Butte Campus Drive, Oroville, CA 95965; (916) 895-2344, fax: (916) 895-2380.

Calhoun Community College, Decatur, Alabama

Calhoun Community College's telecourse program was initiated during the summer quarter of 1991. Since that time, the telecourse program has grown from four course sections enrolling 150 students to approximately 25 to 35 sections per quarter enrolling between 700 to 800 students.

Calhoun's telecourse program now includes 30 PBS courses and, due to the enormous interest from faculty, 22 courses that have been produced by full-time faculty members of the college. Although a few of the telecourses have been offered over public television and local cable networks, the majority of the courses are copied onto videotapes for students to check out of the library and take home for viewing. Currently, Calhoun's library houses 6,000 videotapes that are part of the telecourse program. Faculty interact with students through the use of orientation sessions, voicemail, facsimiles, e-mail, and review sessions.

Contact: Chris Hamilton, Director of Special Projects; Calhoun Community College, P.O. Box 2216, Decatur, AL 35609; (205) 306-2620, fax: (205) 306-2507.

Clovis Community College, Clovis, Minnesota

In partnership with Eastern New Mexico Rural Telephone Cooperative and nine rural school districts, Clovis Community College provides two-way, live interactive higher education programs and services to residents of six counties in eastern New Mexico. Through concurrent high school and college enrollment, the system enriches the curricula of very small rural schools while allowing students to earn college credit. The system also serves place-bound adult students in participating communities.

Clovis Community College offers 88 percent of courses in the New Mexico lower-division general education core and 93 percent of courses needed for A.A. degrees via instructional television. ITV course offerings include one biology course and one physical education activity course adapted for distance delivery.

Contact: David L. Caffey, Dean of Instruction; Clovis Community College, 417 Schepps Blvd., Clovis, NM 88101; (505) 769-4111, fax: (505) 769-4190.

Columbia State Community College, Columbia, Tennessee

The distance learning program at Columbia State encompasses traditional credit courses delivered via interactive compressed video and transmission of live two-way audio, video, and data to three of the college's teaching sites simultaneously. More than 40 contact hours of credit courses are delivered each week on the system, including courses in accounting, business, economics, English, history, humanities, mathematics, and nursing.

Faculty new to the delivery method are provided one-to-one training prior to teaching distance learning class sections and are provided with a handbook containing distance education procedures and guidelines. Evaluation of the distance learning system is conducted at the end of each semester by all faculty and students involved in the classes.

Contact: Betty Kyger, Vice President of Academic Services; Columbia State Community College, P.O. Box 1315, Columbia, TN 38402; (615) 540-2520 ext. 1315, fax: (615) 540-2535.

DeKalb College, Decatur, Georgia

Serving the eastern metropolitan service area of Atlanta, DeKalb College's four learning networks offer numerous options for commuter students. A statewide network of distance learning classrooms that use two-way, interactive television via high-speed telephone lines makes up the Georgia Statewide Academic and Medical System. This network serves the entire state and classrooms are located in colleges and universities, correctional institutions, K–12 schools, and other special sites such as Zoo Atlanta and Georgia Public Television. DeKalb College will soon have electronic compressed video classrooms on each of its five campuses.

A second delivery method is satellite transmission. Currently three campuses form a satellite downlink network and have access to uplink services through Georgia Public Television. Over 30 videoconferences a year provide information that is accessible and cost effective for the institution.

A third delivery method is broadcast and cablecast. Courses are broadcast on WPBA (Channel 30) and cablecast on DeKalb College's Educational Access Channel. These systems serve the metro-Atlanta service area and North Georgia. Classes are aired several times a day and Sunday's lessons are repeat lessons from Saturday's offerings. This same network airs special events and announcements for the community of learners being served.

DeKalb College has joined with six other metro-area University System of Georgia institutions in forming the Metropolitan Atlanta Distance Learning Consortium. The consortium works with private enterprise to develop a microwave/ITFS network that will serve the entire metropolitan Atlanta service area with academic credit courses and continuing education classes.

Contact: Robert R. "Bob" Clark, Distance Learning Coordinator; DeKalb College, 3251 Pantersville Road, Decatur, GA 30034; (404) 244-5013, fax: (404) 244-2996.

Douglas College, New Westminster, British Columbia

The Advanced Diploma program in Psychiatric Nursing at Douglas College, offered in both text-based and online formats, affords registered nurses and registered psychiatric nurses an opportunity to study at an advanced level while continuing to live and work in their home communities. The clinically focused program is equivalent to one year of full-time study and must be completed within five years. Formal clinical placement agreements are established with agencies and organizations relevant to the identified student learning needs through negotiation with an assigned faculty advisor in the Department of Psychiatric Nursing at Douglas College. The program articulates to a Bachelor of Health Science (Psychiatric Nursing) with the Open University of British Columbia.

Contact: Milo Mitchell, Director, Department Psychiatric Nursing; Douglas College, Box 2503 New Westminster, British Columbia, Canada V3L 5B2; (604) 527-5644, fax: (604) 527-5633, URL: http:// www.douglas.bc.ca/psychnur/advdip.html.

Edison Community College, Fort Meyers, Florida

From a beginning enrollment of 600 in 1993–94, Edison Community College's distance learning program grew to 1,700 in 1995–96. Twenty-two telecourses were offered in the fall and spring semesters and an additional eight during the summer term. In the spring semester of 1997, Edison will provide a complete A.A. degree via telecourses.

The uniqueness of the Edison Community College program lies in the outstanding cooperation of WSFP-TV, the local PBS station, which is contributing free air time to foster this effort. Another contributing partner is the Department of Education's ITV Department, which obtains state licensing for many of the telecourses used and offers duplicating services.

Contact: Charles F. Ritchie, Director of Learning Resources; Edison Community College, 8099 College Parkway, SW, Fort Myers, FL 33919; (813) 489-9219, fax: (813) 432-5590.

Herkimer County Community College, Herkimer, New York

The principal goal of Herkimer's Learn Project is to expand educational, vocational, and in-service training opportunities in Herkimer County in rural upstate New York. The distance learning network is a two-way, fully interactive, full-motion video and audio system using fiber-optic cable and telecommunications equipment. Interactive full-motion video and telecommunications technology enables teachers and learners in distance learning classrooms in the high schools and college to see, hear, and talk to students in comparably equipped classrooms on the network. College-credit courses currently offered to high school juniors and seniors, and adult learners are English I and II, Journalism, Mathematical Statistics, Marriage and the Family, National Parks Biology, Introduction to Psychology, Introduction to Sociology, and Spanish I.

Contact: Edward Stone, Coordinator Distance Learning; Herkimer County Community College, Herkimer, NY 13350; (315) 866-0300, fax: (315) 866-7253.

Indian Hills Community College, Ottumwa, Iowa

Indian Hills Community College (IHCC) manages 13 telecommunications classrooms in 10 Southern Iowa counties. All of these classrooms are linked together over the state's fully interactive fiber-optic network (The Iowa Communications Network or ICN). IHCC will be adding an additional six telecommunications classrooms on the Ottumwa Campus, one on the Centerville Campus, and one in each of eight satellite centers. Fourteen additional K–12 sites will be constructed during the 1996–97 school year bringing the future total to 42.

Since the ICN became operational in this part of the state, IHCC has developed a well-rounded distance education program. To assist teachers in feeling comfortable at the podium, IHCC staff members have developed special distance education workshops consisting of three two-hour sessions that combine general distance education information with hands-on experience.

IHCC offers 18 full-term courses through the Arts and Sciences Division. IHCC also has sponsored a number of special events in conjunction with the Continuing Education and Advanced Technology departments as well as other colleges. Special programming was developed and coordinated for the Ottumwa Community Schools Talented and Gifted students.

Contact: Dalas Shockley, Dean, Learning Resources; Indian Hills Community College, 525 Grandview Avenue, Ottumwa, IA 52501; (515) 683-5174, fax: (515) 683-5184.

Iowa Valley Community College District, Marshalltown, Iowa

The distance education program offered by the Iowa Valley Community College District (IVCCD) is delivered by the state fiber-optics telecommunications network. The district has two campuses separated by a distance of 60 miles: Marshalltown Community College in Marshalltown and Ellsworth Community College in Iowa Falls. The ICN spans that distance and makes it possible for the two community colleges to share a variety of courses through a medium that offers full-color, full-motion, two-way interactive audio and video.

Contact: John S. Erwin, Dean of Instruction, Marshalltown Community College; Iowa Valley Community College District, 3700 S. Center Street, Marshalltown, IA 50158; (515) 752-7106, fax: (515) 752-8149.

LakeShore Technical College, Cleveland, Wisconsin

LakeShore Technical College (LTC) in east-central Wisconsin offers a nine-month Pharmacy Technical diploma program using distance learning technologies. Students learn in classrooms and pharmacies using local hospital facilities and equipment in 12 sites up to 150 miles from LTC. The didactic instruction is provided via transmissions from LTC over a television/telephone interactive network. Local technical colleges in participating areas provide the general education components of the program.

The technologies used include AT&T Picasso still-frame technology, instructional television fixed service (ITFS), and telephone. The program model has also been used for other LTC programs.

Contact: James Malmberg, Administrator Institutional Research and Distance Learning; LakeShore Technical College, 1290 North Avenue, Cleveland, WI 53015; (414) 458-4183 ext. 131, fax: (414) 457-6211.

Lethbridge Community College, Lethbridge, Alberta

Prior to the development of the Center for Distance Education development at Lethbridge Community College (LCC), four distinct programs relied on their own limited resources to facilitate the distance learning process. Upon development of the center, resources were centralized and made available to other programs which wanted to develop distance education delivery strategies.

The center resulted in the development of delivery standards, increased responsiveness to learner needs, increased opportunity for expansion, and better evaluation and developmental techniques, while effectively using the college's limited resources.

Contact: Alan Stephen, Manager, Center for Distance Education; Lethbridge Community College, 3000 College Drive South, Lethbridge, AB Canada T1K1L6; (403) 320-3235, fax: (403) 380-4464.

Los Angeles Community College District, Los Angeles, California

Instructional Television is the districtwide, distance learning program of the nine-college Los Angeles Community College District, serving 4,000 to 5,000 students each year in an area covering over 415 square miles.

Instructors come to the central ITV office one afternoon and one evening weekly to interact with students by phone, mail, voicemail, and in person. Instructors also offer four weekend seminars of three hours each at at least two colleges. An orientation, which includes a study skills review for distance learning, is offered to students at the beginning of each semester at four colleges over a two-day weekend.

A group enrollment program is available for groups of 15 or more students at a school or work site who want to enroll in the same telecourse. Videotapes are loaned to such groups and instructor may be available to meet with groups. Customized viewing schedules are developed for groups so that they meet midterm and final deadlines.

Contact: Paul G. McKenna, Director; Los Angeles Community College District, 855 North Vermont Avenue, Los Angeles, CA 90029; (213) 953-4488, fax: (213) 666-4042.

Mount Royal College, Calgary, Alberta

The Post Basic Mental Health Nursing program and Gerontology Certificate program at Mount Royal College feature both independent and interactive components: comprehensive print-based materials, designated instructor-student teaching hours, audio-teleconferences, on-campus workshops, e-mail and selected audio-visual materials. The role of the teacher and the distance team is shaped by the underlying philosophical belief that student-teacher relationships are key to the educational process and that learning is a collaborative, shared experience. Teaching strategies focus on creatively connecting with students to support and facilitate learning endeavors.

The courses in these programs have transfer credit to Alberta Universities and are designed for individuals who already hold a diploma, associate degree, or degree. Students enroll from across Canada and the United States. In 1995, the Center for Health Studies expanded to include two additional distance programs: Neonatal Intensive Care Nursing and Advanced Studies in Critical Care Nursing.

Contact: Sharon Moore, Coordinator of Post Basic Mental Health Nursing Program; Center for Health Studies, Mount Royal College, 4825 Richard Road SW, Calgary, Alberta Canada T3E 6K6; 1-800-240-6891, fax: (403) 240-6203; URL: http://www.mtroyal.ab.ca.

New Brunswick Community College, Moncton, New Brunswick

The New Brunswick Provincial Correspondence Service is operated from the New Brunswick Community College campus at Moncton. This service provides learning opportunities chiefly to New Brunswick residents but is open to anyone, offering 33 courses from grades 7–12 in an individualized learning format. Students may start a course at any time. These credits are primarily used to complete high school, and to fulfill prerequisites for entrance to a college or university program.

Contact: Joy Stuart, Distance Education Officer; New Brunswick Community College-Moncton, 1234 Mountain Road, Moncton, NB, Canada E1C 8H9; (506) 856-2237, (506) 856-3288; e-mail: jstuart@mctmail.nbnet.nb.ca.

Northcentral Technical College, Wausau, Wisconsin

Northcentral Technical College (NTC) has developed a telecommunications system to deliver educational services to regional campuses, K–12 schools, business and industry, and other educational institutions throughout the state and nation. The system is multifaceted and integrates several different technologies to deliver voice, video, and data services. NTC uses point-to-point microwave, ITFS (omnidirectional microwave), T-1, and fiber-optic (full DS-3) for its Interactive television system (ITV). This system has the capability to deliver six ITV courses simultaneously to multiple receive sites in full two-way video and audio. NTC's ITV system is unique in Wisconsin and it comparable to only a few other systems in the United States.

NTC's ITV system provides access districtwide to its programs. A student may complete the Accounting, Supervisory Management, Industrial Engineering, or Information Processing Specialist program at a regional campus. Other programs using ITV include Administrative Assistant, Farm Business and Production, Marketing, Nursing, and Police Science. In 1995–96, 173 courses were delivered serving 4,025 students. Over 50 percent of those students were distance learners.

Initially NTC's ITV system was developed to extend its classrooms and instructional expertise throughout the district. Today, NTC is sharing its unique programs statewide through a multi-institutional fiber-optic network.

Contact: Barb Cummings, Associate Dean of Alternative Delivery Systems; Northcentral Technical College, 1000 W. Campus Drive, Wausau, WI 54401-1899; (715) 675-3331, fax: (715) 675-9776; e-mail: cummings/ntc@mail.northcentral.tec.wi.us.

Open College, Open Learning Agency, Burnaby, British Columbia

The Dental Assisting Program is offered through a combination of open learning methods such as print, audiotape, videotape, audio conferencing, and face-to-face clinical courses. The theory is delivered throughout British Columbia solely using distance education and tutors who support students by telephone and mail. Clinical courses are offered in different leased dental clinics in a variety of locations. Integration of clinical and theory is accomplished as all students are employed as chairside assistants while they are enrolled. Graduates of the program are registered and licensed certified dental assistants.

With federal funding, the Open College modified and adapted the existing distance program and offered a full-time version to a selected group of 20 students living in five remote communities. It was still offered in a distance format, but study groups in the communities were formed, additional teleconferences were held, instructors were flown to the communities for a series of one week instructional and supervisional visits, and students progressed through the program as a cohort, rather than independently.

The project demonstrated that a full-time program could be delivered by distance as a project to meet community needs. No buildings were built, no equipment was required, and no infrastructure was created.

Contact: Debbie Payne, Coordinator, Dental Programs and Projects; Open College, 4355 Mathissi Place, Burnaby, B.C. Canada V5G 4S8; (604) 431-3207, fax: (604) 431-3387; e-mail: debbiep@ola.bc.ca.

Owens Community College, Toledo, Ohio

Ameritech, the Ohio Manufacturer's Association (OMA), and Owens Community College have partnered to bring Skill Link to the Ohio communities of Toledo and Findlay. Six companies were selected to represent Ohio's manufacturing community. Skill Link is supported by a grant from Ameritech and is managed by Owens Community College. The network simulates a live classroom experience using a two-way, full-color, full-motion, interactive video system transmitted over a public fiber-optic network. Multiple instructional support systems are incorporated at all sites. Additionally, the network is connected to the Findlay City Schools.

The network provides business with a means of delivering college courses directly to the work place on a cost-effective basis and connects the college, schools, and industry into one network to effectively deliver limited instructional resources simultaneously to multiple locations. The system has been used to offer apprenticeship training, developmental and technical education, computer training, business management, and a complete first-line supervision certificate program including "graduation" over the system. Plans are developing to link the system to the Toledo City Fire Division to bring firefighter training to fire stations. Other businesses are actively investigating participation.

The Skill Link project is intended to be a model for the development of similar networks with design improvements based on pilot project experiences to be made in future installations. The college recently received a $300,000 Ohio Board of Regents Productivity Improvements Challenge grant to continue and expand the network.

Contact: Paul V. Unger, Vice President for Academic Affairs; Owens Community College, P.O. Box 10,000, Toledo, OH 43699; (419) 661-7250, fax: (419) 661-7366; e-mail: punger@toledolink.com.

Piedmont Technical College, Greenwood, South Carolina

In order to meet urgent education and training needs in its seven-county service area, Piedmont Technical College is implementing a full-motion, interactive audio and video, fiber-optic distance learning delivery system. The system will be compatible with the SCETV satellite system and will adhere to national standards for audio and video transmission via fiber telephone lines. When completed, this system will provide access via a full fiber link among seven counties within the college service area. Each location will have a distance learning room with three cameras controlled by the instructor (front, rear, and overhead) and television monitors showing four locations when needed, plus. a synchronized input source for videotape and computer generated signals.

In addition to the video and audio transmissions, each distance learning room will be linked to the main campus networks. Access to the library's online public access catalog, training resource center, and extensive CD-ROM information collection will be accessed by computers in each distance learning room. Access to necessary basic skills software will also be available from a simple menu selection on the room's computers.

This system will use Asynchronous Transfer Mode (ATM) services for data and video transmission. Motion Picture Experts Group (MPEG) or MPEG2 compression standards will be used to keep the bandwidth requirements at a minimum. The college will work with a consortium of entities to secure the fiber-optic cable necessary for the system. These entitles include local government agencies, cable companies and telephone companies. In addition to the college, users of the system will be a local university and six area school districts.

Contact: Thomas V. Mecca, Vice President for Educational Affairs; Piedmont Technical College, Post Office Box 1467, Greenwood, SC 29648; (863) 941-8307, fax: (863) 941-8555.

Pima Community College, Tucson, Arizona

The distance education program at Pima Community College is composed of two facets; telecourses and classes offered via interactive classrooms. Each semester, up to 30 courses are broadcast over four cable networks to the general community. Subject areas include anthropology, business, computer science, history, literature, mathematics, psychology, Spanish, and writing. Telecourse presentations may include lecture as well as prerecorded video packages.

Assessment of the efficacy of the telecourses is a current project of the college. Data from telecourse offerings will be compared with data collected on the same classes offered in the "traditional" classroom format. The results of this study will be used to increase the effectiveness of the distance learning program.

Three of the branch campuses have recently been linked by an interactive classroom set-up and a fourth branch will be added to the network shortly. This network will be used for both instructional purposes as well as for meetings involving representatives from the various campuses. The large size (over 9,100 square miles) of Pima County offers special challenges as well as incentives for this type of program.

Contact: Martin Sade, Department Chair, Mathematics; Pima Community College, 1901 N. Stone Avenue, Tucson, AZ 85709; (520) 884-6488, fax: (520) 884-6288.

Portland Community College, Portland, Oregon

Portland Community College uses videocassettes, cable, ITFS, satellite links, compressed video, audio conferencing, modems, and the Internet to provide credit and noncredit instruction and services to distance students in the three-county district, and to students throughout Oregon. The college Tel-Net connects over 50 sites in a teleconference network.

Distance Learning reaches over 5,000 students annually with telecourses, live televised instruction, and online courses. The college is a participant in "Going the Distance," the PBS distance education degree initiative. The college's dial-in registration system, online library access, and web site all support distance learners.

Contact: John Sneed; Portland Community College, PO Box 19000, CC 220 Sylvania, Portland, OR 97280-0990; (503)977-4398, fax: (503)977-4858; e-mail: JSneed@pcc.edu.

Raritan Valley Community College, Somerville, New Jersey

The three-credit course "Internet Navigation" is driven by electronic mail and online searches on the Internet. It was offered for the first time as a distance learning course during spring semester 1995 and enrolled 21 students. The course instructs students in the use of local and global networks and provides hands-on experience accessing and retrieving information and software from Internet and other electronic catalogs. With the exception of an initial on-campus session, students work independently from homes or work sites.

Contact: Charlotte Ravitz, Dean of Instruction; Raritan Valley Community College, P.O. Box 3300, Somerville, NJ 08876; (908) 526-1200 ext. 8294, fax: (908) 526-0253.

Red Deer College, Red Deer, Alberta

A joint project of three Alberta Colleges: Red Deer College, Kayas Cultural College, and Fairview College, the Northern Teacher Assistant program is one of the first in the province to use videoconferencing to deliver educational programming. The program is offered in three northern communities: Jean D'Or Prairie, Fox Lake, and Garden River (the Little Red River Cree Nation). Instructors teach in one locale and the program is delivered via videoconferencing to the other two communities. Face-to-face contact between instructors and students is facilitated by instructors traveling to and teaching in each of the three communities on a rotational basis.

Core courses offered in the Red Deer College Teacher Assistant program are offered, as well as optional courses including Cree Syllabics, Native Studies, Team Building, and Special Education, which were developed to meet the needs of the local communities.

This project is one step towards the Little Red River Cree Nation's goals to have locally trained First Nations teachers in its nation-run school system. Discussions are currently underway with a number of universities to facilitate transferability of the

Teacher Assistant program to a Bachelor of Education program. Other First Nation Education Authorities are examining this model for delivery of postsecondary training to northern aboriginal communities.

Contact: Linda Moreau, Chairperson, Teacher Assistant Program; Red Deer College, Box 5005, Red Deer, AB, Canada T4N 5H5; (403) 342-3300, fax: (403) 340-8940.

Red Rocks Community College, Lakewood, Colorado

Red Rocks Community College's distance education program (LET) has made over 100 courses available to some 1,000 students since 1992. The hallmarks of the system are a concern for rural education, attention to the details of curriculum design and instruction, and extensive support services for faculty and others teaching over the LET. The program provides up to 30 hours of customized training for those teaching over the system, and features hands-on equipment practice as well as general teaching theory and an emphasis on interactive strategies. An instructional designer, a distance education specialist, and a multimedia developer provide support services during and after training.

Contact: John O'Neill, Telecommunications Technician and Distance Education Specialist; Red Rocks Community College, 13300 West Sixth Avenue Box 37, Lakewood, CO 80401; (303) 914-6303, fax: (303) 989-6919.

Rockland Community College, Suffern, New York

Rockland Community College (RCC) offers 34 semester-bound telecourses (14 during the summer session and two during the winter), and 17 rolling-admission distance learning courses.

The program offers students an opportunity to obtain an Associate in Liberal Arts degree. As part of the State University of New York (SUNY) system, an RCC A.A. degree is accepted by all SUNY four-year colleges and universities. In addition, many private four-year colleges also accept these courses for credit.

Videotapes accompanying each course may be viewed in the media center weekdays and Saturdays. They are also aired on the cable channel, TKR, and on the New Jersey Network, WNJN. In addition, students can borrow videotapes for home viewing. Each course is mentored by a faculty member available to students by telephone or in face-to-face meetings. The Department of Instructional Technology supervises all daily procedural activities and assists in ensuring the program's continuing success.

Contact: Fleur Eshghi, Director, Instructional Technology Center; Rockland Community College, 145 College Road, Suffern, NY 10901; (914) 574-4732, fax: (914) 356-5811.

Sault College of Applied Arts and Technology, Sault Ste. Marie, Ontario

The Aboriginal Resource Technician program provides a unique opportunity for aboriginal persons located across Northern Ontario to achieve the formal qualifications necessary to obtain permanent employment with private industry, a natural resources employer, Lands and Tribal Councils, or other government agencies. The distance education program offers 32 courses meant to span a three-year period. The majority of the courses concentrate in the area of forestry but include business, English, mathematics, native studies, and science. A student's weekly commitment includes eight to 10 hours of scheduled teleconferencing, home study, and two days of work placement with a sponsoring employer. Certain components of the program are completed on site at Sault College during one of two sessions scheduled during the year.

The program is delivered using the Contact North Network. When students meet with faculty for the online sessions, they have access to self-study guides, an electronic blackboard, facsimile machines, videotapes, audiotapes, and computers. In some courses, study specimens and lab kits are sent to each site.

Contact: Cora Hennel-Greer, Coordinator, Curriculum Development and Instructional Design; Sault College of Applied Arts and Technology, P.O. Box 60, 443 Northern Avenue, Sault Ste. Marie, ON P6A 5L3; (705) 759-2554 ext. 597, fax: (705) 759-1319; e-mail: corah@opc.saultc.on.ca, URL: http://www.saultc.on.ca.

Sierra Community College, Rocklin, California

Sierra Community College has designed an affordable distance learning system by partnering with local cable companies. The district (nearly 3,000 square miles) transmits signals via microwave to five different cable systems allowing the college to offer courses to students at home via television. Students at home communicate live with instructors and classmates by telephone. Currently, 13 courses are broadcast over a 42-hour period weekly.

Contact: Suzanne Devenport, Multimedia Program, Production and Design Specialist; Sierra Community College, 5000 Rocklin Road, Rocklin, CA 95677; (916) 789-2638, fax: (916) 789-2632.

South Metropolitan Regional Higher Education Consortium, University Park, Illinois

The South Metropolitan Regional Higher Education Consortium, one of 10 regional consortia in Illinois, is organized to bring together resources to promote new and enhanced educational services and programs to citizens, businesses and other institutions in its region. Members include community colleges, public and private colleges, and universities located south-southwest of Chicago. The Consortium operates a 27-site interactive distance education network with two-way audio/video compressed video technology. The network provides gateways within and beyond the state using a variety of technologies. Sites include main and satellite campuses of its members, rural high schools, and a hospital.

Contact: Margaret M. Donohue, Consortium Director; South Metropolitan Regional Higher Education Consortium, Governors State University, University Park, IL 60466; (708) 534-4495, fax: (708) 534-8458.

State Community College of East Saint Louis, East Saint Louis, Illinois

State Community College has a Distance Learning College with two sections: Video Correspondence and Interactive Video. Both offer residents of metro East Saint Louis (and through interactive T-1 lines, residents of southern Illinois south of I-70) the opportunity to earn college credit by taking college courses over WSCC-TV's cable channel, over interactive video T-1 lines, or by cassette tape check-out. Credits earned are applied to the college's degree or certificate program. The Distance Learning College offers its consortial members a variety of niche courses such as Minority Issues & the Economic Order, Black Studies, Religious Studies, Addiction Counseling, and Environmental Science Technology.

The Video Correspondence section had developed over a five-year period and now accounts for over 20 percent of the college's enrollment. Seventy percent of the correspondence students live within the district. Over half of the students in the video correspondence section are full-time workers; many of the rest work part time. Forty percent report they are shift workers which prevents them from taking scheduled on-campus classes. Nearly 75 percent of the students in this section are women.

WSCC-TV (Channel 12) provides information about the Distance Learning College to its cable subscribers. It also offers a one-hour daily airing of telecourses for those students who do not have access to a VCR or whose equipment malfunctions. WSCC-TV is scheduled to provide GED instruction for a large number of the estimated 4,400 people in East Saint Louis who need the GED certificate. Cable drop-lines are being installed to key centers in the city's housing projects, to the Senior Citizen Center, to public aid offices, and other important locations.

Contact: W. J. van Grunsven, Director, Distance Learning College; State Community College of East Saint Louis, Governor James R. Thompson Boulevard, East Saint Louis, IL 62201; (618) 583-2568 or 583-2573, fax: (618) 583-2526.

University College of the Fraser Valley, Abbotsford, British Columbia

University College of the Fraser Valley (UCFV) has an established virtual classroom program which offers students an opportunity to earn college credit by taking courses via home computers. Currently the credits earned are applied to an existing diploma or degree program offered within the various career or academic departments.

UCFV expects to offer 15 to 18 online courses in the 1996 fall and winter semesters and five courses during spring semester 1997. The college uses the FirstClass™ conferencing system available for both Windows and Macintosh systems. Generally, online students are working adults who appreciate the time flexibility of the courses as well as the savings in travel costs.

Contact: Patrick O'Brien, Director, UCFV On-Line; University College of Fraser Valley, Abbotsford Campus, 33844 King Rd., RR #2, Abbotsford, B.C., Canada V2S 7M9; (604) 853-7441, fax: (604) 855-7558; e-mail: obrien@ucfv.bc.ca.

University of Alaska Southeast, Sitka, Alaska

The Associate of Applied Science degree in Health Information Management (HIM) was the first degree program approved by the University of Alaska Board of Regents for distance delivery. The HIM program was implemented in the fall of 1992, and graduated its first students in 1995. The program is accredited by the Northwest Association of Schools and Colleges and the American Health Information Management Association.

In March 1995, the HIM program was selected by the Western Interstate Cooperative on Higher Education to participate in a telecommunications education brokering project. The objective of the project was to assist consortium institutions in offering programs across state lines. The UAS HIM program began delivery to selected sites in Wyoming in fall 1995, and offered the program to students in New Mexico in fall 1996.

Using a variety of distance technology—primarily audioconferencing with audio/videotape and computer-assisted backup—students complete HIM-specific courses in their home communities. UAS encourages students to complete general education requirements at a local campus, if available, but also distance-delivers general education requirements to those students who do not have such access. Designed to serve remote and widely dispersed communities, almost all student-instructor contact is via telephone, e-mail, and fax. The university has also established a network of distance coordinators in multiple communities so that students have a local contact.

Contact: Carol Petrie Liberty, MS, RRA, Assistant Professor/HIM Program Director; University of Alaska Southeast, 1332 Seward Avenue, Sitka, AK 99835-9498; (907) 747-6653, (907) 747-3552.

University of Cincinnati, Cincinnati, Ohio

The Open Learning Fire Service Program (OLFSP) affords active-duty fire service personnel an opportunity to earn credit toward an associate degree in Fire Science Technology and a bachelor's degree in Fire and Safety Engineering Technology. Fire service courses are taken by correspondence. Modes of contact include mail, fax, and the Internet. Students are encouraged to contact instructors with questions or concerns.

The University of Cincinnati's OLFSP offers over 17 fire courses covering topics including: Fire Tactics, Hazardous Materials, Advance Fire Administration, Fire Prevention Organization and Management, Fire Protection Structure and Systems Design, Disaster and Fire Defense Planning, Personnel Management, Incendiary Fire Analysis, and Fire Dynamics. Students may also pursue courses in mathematics, computer science, humanities, and technical electives through open learning or at a local college or university.

Contact: Patrick T. Reynolds, Department Head; University of Cincinnati, 2220 Victory Parkway, Cincinnati, OH 45206-2822; (513) 556-6583, fax: (513) 556-4856.

Waubonsee Community College, Sugar Grove, Illinois

Waubonsee Community College is entering its second decade of offering two-way, interactive television courses via a network that includes microwave, satellite, T-1, and DS-3 transmission.

Four community colleges, four private colleges and universities, and two public universities have partnered with Waubonsee to provide credit and noncredit training via the Distance Learning Network. Currently the network offers over 120 college courses and seminars each year. In addition to coursework, the network is used by the business community for specialized courses and satellite programming. Since its inception, over 6,000 students have participated in courses offered via the distance learning network.

Contact: Lynn Murphy, Dean of Learning Resources and Instructional Technology; Waubonsee Community College, Rt. 47 @ Harter Road, Sugar Grove, IL 60554; (630) 466-4811, ext. 2378, fax: (630) 466-7799; e-mail: lynnm@wccb.wcc.cc.il.us.

Wayne County Community College, Detroit, Michigan

Wayne County Community College has been offering telecourses to its students since 1978 and was one of the first "Going the Distance" institutions. Initially focusing on general education courses, the program has been expanded to provide students with the opportunity to complete an Associate of Arts or Associate of General Studies degree with an emphasis in business. Twenty to twenty-five courses are offered each fall and spring term, and approximately 10 courses are offered during a 10-week accelerated summer term.

All courses offered each semester are available on the college's cable channel (programmed through a local educational consortium) and transmitted by ITFS signal to participating cable company head-ends; selected courses are also broadcast by the local PBS station. Periodic on-campus class sessions are required and are scheduled evenings and Saturdays to allow maximum flexibility for students, who may attend class sessions at either campus or switch back and forth between campuses as needed. In most instances, full-time faculty have been recruited to develop and teach the telecourses offered. Certification training is required of all faculty wishing to teach existing telecourses.

A 24-hour, 7-day Telecourse Hotline is available for students needing to contact faculty or staff between on-campus class sessions. Faculty are provided with all necessary clerical and administrative support to provide distance learning students with a positive academic experience.

Contact: Deborah Fiedler, Manager, Instructional Telecommunications; Wayne County Community College, 801 W. Fort Street, Detroit, MI 48226; (313) 496-2602, fax: (313) 496-0451; e-mail: citcdf@admin.wccc.edu.

Wisconsin Indianhead Technical College, Shell Lake, Wisconsin

Wisconsin Indianhead Technical College (WITC) provides flexible education linking business and education for employment in a service area one-fifth the land area of Wisconsin. Through instructional television, about 500 people in Northwest Wisconsin participate annually in approximately 30 courses. Courses are credit and noncredit: some apply toward an associate degree or certificate program; others are customized to meet employers' workplace needs.

From its beginning, WITC's ITV networks have exemplified education-business government partnerships. NWECS was the first network in the country in which local phone companies provided educators with a single point of contact, funded by multiple education, government, and private funding sources. An historic 1992 launch featured Governor Thompson interacting from hundreds of miles away with WITC, K–12, agency, and university partners, as well as legislators and local officials. Highlights of the system are:

- Northern Wisconsin Educational Communications System (NWECS). Single-channel fiber-optic system. Sixteen sites: four WITC campuses, one administrative office; seven secondary school districts; La Courte Oreilles Community College; Cooperative Educational Services Agency 12; and University of Wisconsin-Superior.
- Western Wisconsin Instructional Network Group (WestWING). Fiber-optic system of 11 high school sites, WITC-New Richmond, and UW-River Falls. WITC-New Richmond provides ITV courses and meetings for NWECS and WestWING.
- Wisconsin Indianhead Narrowcast (WIN) network microwave systems links communities and five high school districts in Rusk County with WITC-Rice Lake.
- Indianhead Distance Learning Consortium is in development for certain schools in Washbrun, Burnett, Polk, and Barron counties. WITC supports this consortium.
- WITC is capable of connecting with Wisconsin Overlay Network of Distance Learning Education Resources (WONDER), a fiber link between four Wisconsin Technical Colleges and five University of Wisconsin campuses.

Contact: David R. Hildebrand, President; Wisconsin Indianhead Technical College, 505 Pine Ridge Drive, Shell Lake, WI 54871; (715) 468-2815, fax: (715) 468-2819.

SELECTED BIBLIOGRAPHY

Bates, A.W. (1995). *Technology, Open Learning, and Distance Education*. New York: Routledge.

Burge, Elizabeth J. and Howard, Joan L. "Audio-Conferencing in Graduate Education: A Case Study." *American Journal of Distance Education*, 4(2), 3–13.

Conway, Paul. "Voice Networking: Big Technology on Campus." *THE Journal*, 17(8), 67– 68.

Hannu, R.W. "Interactive Television Networking." *THE Journal*, 17(8), 60–62.

Hutcher, Peter. "SchoolLink: Telecommunications Transforms Distance Learning." *THE Journal,* 17(9), 72–74.

Lever-Duffy, Judy. (1991). *Distance Education Resource Guide*. Mission Viejo, California: League for Innovation in the Community College.

Kelly, Henry. "Technology and the Transformation of American Education." *THE Journal,* 18(1), 60–63.

Kurshan, Barbara. "Creating the Global Classroom for the 21st Century." *Educational Technology.* 31(4), 47–50.

Portway, Patrick S. and Lane, Carla. eds. (1994). *Teleconferencing and Distance Learning.* San Ramon, California: Applied Business Telecommunications

Reed, Diane and Sork, Thomas. "Ethical Consideration in Distance Education." *American Journal of Distance Education,* 4(2), 30–43.

Rogers, E.M. (1986). *Communications Technology: The New Media in Society.* New York: Free Press.

Solomon, Martin B. "E-Mail: A Primer for Academics." *THE Journal*, 18(1), 64–65.

Verduin, John R. and Clark, Thomas A. (1991). *Distance Education: The Foundations of Effective Practice.* San Francisco: Jossey-Bass.

Ward, Jaci. "Landline Two-Way Video: Being There and Here." *THE Journal,* 17(9), 59–61.

Willis, Barry. (1993*). Distance Education: A Practical Guide*. Englewood Cliffs, New Jersey: Educational Technology Publications.